# Putting Power In Your Perceptions

## A Practical Guide To Greater Effectiveness

Dr. Ray Watson

RJW Publications
Bellevue, Washington

*Copyright 1995 by Dr. Ray Watson*
*All rights reserved*
*Printed in U.S.A.*
*Library of Congress Catalog 94-78434*
*ISBN 0-9635686-0-4*


This book may not be reproduced in whole or in part, by mimeograph or any other means, without permission. For information contact:


**RJW Publications**
P. O. Box 40190
**Bellevue, Washington 98015-4190**

## **Dedication**

*To my mother, Dorothy ...*
*and that indomitable spirit*
*that doesn't know what it cannot do.*

## *Acknowledgements*

Any personal achievement is only a reflection of what has been given to us, and what we have chosen to do with it. This book is no less. I gratefully acknowledge what has been given to me by my many clients, colleagues, friends; those who have blessed me beyond my imagination, and those who have enriched my experience in life by less than pleasant means. Understanding the dynamics and power of perceptions is born from receiving what I have hoped for, dreaded, and at times not understood. Learning about the tools to more effectively manage our lives, whatever the focus or direction, is the net result of the blessings of the good, the bad, and the ugly. The reasons behind the intentions of those who contribute to those experiences doesn't really matter. They are no less than the necessary components for the opportunity to learn to live with great vitality, fervor, and hope.

From a practical side, I am deeply indebted to a couple who, beyond their professional role in producing this book, have also added much to the color of my life. Thorn and Ursula Bacon, of BestSeller Consultants, have been there as patient and competent guides to bring to fullfillment the always more than expected challenges of creating a book and bringing it to the marketplace. Their friendship is a benchmark of my passage to an expanded focus of the direction of my living.

Dr. Ray Watson

## *Table of Contents*

  Introduction ........................................... vi

**Part I**
1. Deliberate Detours ................................ 1
2. Perceptions For New Directions .................... 23
3. Choosing The View That Creates The Outcomes ...... 37
4. Winning At Making Failure Unnecessary ............ 51
5. Why We Are Where We Are: Choices That Create A Way Of Living ................................. 67
6. Power Brokering; The Use And Balance Of Personal Power .................................. 77

**Part II**

7. The Deciding Force ............................... 95
8. Freedom To Choose A Narrow Road ................. 103
9. A Perspective On Values ......................... 129
10. Feeling And Focus ............................... 141
11. Intimacy, Problem Solving And Other Crises ...... 159
12. The Unfamiliar Friend ........................... 169
  Conclusion ..................................... 183

## *Introduction*

Given the myriad of situations that define our lives differently from one another, one underlying encounter confronts everyone similarly. This challenge pivots around the perceptions of the experiences we have — how we look at what is occurring — and has a profound impact on the degree to which the experience impales or pushes us, helps or hinders our lives at that time.

These perceptions we carry with us are learned … learned ways of looking at the things that occur. This book is an invitation to recognize how much influence those perceptions have over how we are affected by whatever occurs. It is also an opportunity to learn how to put power — influence to our benefit and well being — into the way we look at the good, the bad, the unknown, and the hoped for that take place in the course of living.

It seems to me that getting through life takes far more energy than it should. Most of us are too busy managing the demands of day-to-day life to actually enjoy life fully. This book is not a protest of that reality, but rather an invitation to explore ideas that enable us not to have to work quite so hard in trying to accomplish a quality of life that appeals to us.

As a practicing psychotherapist, I come into contact with people daily who are overcome with stress, strain and confusion. This allows me to watch and learn from those with whom I have the unusual privilege of entering a personal world, and to share in the sacred search toward more effective living. Sometimes this process is nothing more than removing the self created obstacles. Frequently it involves clarifying what we are trying to accomplish in any number of situations, and how to more effectively manage the process.

It is always of interest to me while observing normal people with normal life problems as to why there are often such significantly different outcomes for different people. These are similar people with similar abilities who possess the talent to meet their individual challenges. The results range from miserable failure to outrageous success.

It is to this consideration that this book is addressed. All of us want to be more effective in our work and in the pleasant business of living a life. And all of us are acquainted with people who seem to be able to make their plans come true with no more effort than the ones who fail. What makes the difference? The difference is a matter of how we tend to look at our experiences. In other words, it isn't what happens to us that is so important, but how we look at it, perceive its meaning, and then respond to it. The process of getting to our goals, whether they are the personal quality of life, business or professional achievements, or overcoming any kind of setback, all are reduced to one simple process — the unconsciously developed way of perceiving things. The other side of that equation is in learning how to put power into the way we may choose to look at our experiences which will have a significant impact on the eventual outcome.

Your will see from reading the stories of those who have been successful, and those who have failed, how that your patterns of perception are either a helpful and inspiring friend, or a voice whose view of things is a corrosive message which undermines what might otherwise easily be accomplished.

This book will help you identify the reasons successful people accomplish what they do, and why those who, in spite of great effort and intention, are confused and disappointed in the results they experience. By understanding this, we can make the effort that we put into any aspect of our living more effective. You'll discover that the major difference between your personal success or failure living your life will be greatly affected by how you perceive the situations you experience. Your perception of any event, goal, idea, dream, accomplishment or failure, will, to a remarkable extent, dictate the eventual outcome. We will not overlook the realities that challenge us to the limits of human endurance, those things over which we often have no control. Rather we will focus on developing the ability to view those events and to respond in a way that will give us much more positive control of the outcome.

You will also discover here more efficient and effective ways of accomplishing the results you want to achieve. Whether your objective is to create lasting personal change, or to continue to fine-tune what already works for you, you are either launching or continuing a process that will enhance every area of your life.

This is a book about living effectively. In contrast to existing, living is the task of putting all of the desired pieces of life together and learning how to manage those pieces to function in harmony. It is also learning the skills of managing the unexpected, the dreaded, the hoped for, and the dreams themselves once they are in our grasp.

# Part

# I

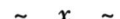

# 1

## *Deliberate Detours*

This is a book for dreamers, visionaries, competitors, entrepreneurs, patients in recovery, victims of crime—virtually anyone who wants to get to a different place in his life and learn to have the power to influence the outcome of the events that occur to live more effectively. The ideas I want to share are not presented to challenge the solid values you have achieved in learning to be satisfied and fulfilled with part or all of your present life. Rather, this book is a vehicle to show you how not to settle, be complacent, or resigned to an unsatisfactory existence that falls short of how you would rather be living. Perhaps this book will help to clear up the confusion you may have about yourself and why you haven't achieved what you dream of doing. Most of all, you will be given some additional tools that will give you a greater sense of power to manage your goals and ambitions with a greater degree of effectiveness.

In working with people in such contrasting experiences in their lives, I am always looking for themes. Themes that can tell me about the freedoms or limitations people experience when they encounter events and circumstances. This includes how we respond behaviorally, emotionally, and probably, most importantly, perceptually. Amazingly, two people who experience the identical situation, hear the same conversation, see the same event take place, may later report entirely different versions of what happened. We've all heard it said ... "Well, it depends on how you look at it."

How we interpret something we witness is based largely on the attitudes, personal experiences, views, and beliefs we have accumulated in a lifetime. In this sense, there is no such thing as purely objective reporting of an experience. Our perception of the event is colored by an almost infinite variety of past experiences, views, beliefs and present needs. The more we subconsciously believe the event may have a direct impact on us, the greater the likelihood that our view of the event will be distorted. Because of having become so sensitized to the distorted observations of clients in my practice, I am often wonderfully entertained by my own shortcomings in the honest interpretation of things that happen to me.

As an example, when my 45th birthday was looming on my personal horizon, I decided to give some extra effort to staying in better physical condition. I already was riding my horses, cleaning stalls, working on my home, skiing and generally staying quite active, but I wanted something more aerobic. I absolutely hate indoor static exercise, so much to my delight I discovered an advertisement for a local rowing club at one of our smaller regional lakes. Two weeks later found me on the water, confirming several things: It was good therapy being on the water; the exercise was great; a few lessons would certainly help, and the water is cold in March.

Rowing is one of those sports created to be watched. There is something intriguing and mystical about those early morning pictures of the fog-shrouded scull slicing through glassy smooth waters, outlined by the dual rings of long oars kissing the water, urging forward this fragile sculpture faster than it should be able.

Whether one's experience rowing matches this description depends on the perceptual process. Before getting on the water, all of the components of rowing are assembled for the perceptions to evaluate. The size of the shell, including that narrow, round bottom — read: *Totally* unstable. How many other rowers are around, and for which Ivy

League Crew they rowed. The water conditions. How long it has been since the last time out. What is the wind doing: How the last experience went, etc., etc,. etc. As a new rower back then, those things all demanded my attention. My rate of developing expertise in a skinny, unstable shell depended largely on what I did with those things I had to process.

Each of those components of the rowing experience, depending on how they were looked at, could inspire either fear, intimidation, challenge or determination. The issue here is not what you have to deal with getting to ready to row, but *how* you will *choose* to look at what is being presented. To become an accomplished rower demands more than bravado.

My rowing instructor told me that women often made better rowers, or at least they learn faster than men. His point was well taken: "Women listen and are not afraid to take instruction to learn the techniques that are essential. Men try to get out there and muscle their way through it." I knew he was right when I watched a well built Marine take a shell out one afternoon. After struggling his way out a few hundred feet from shore, I watched him lose his tan while arms and legs flailed around trying desperately to stay balanced. He made it back to the dock, but later discreetly asked me for a few pointers. I gave him the "get a few lessons" routine, but his perceptual system which looked at things from a "Stronger-is-Better" view just didn't want to see it differently. He didn't notice the skinny 80-year-old man whiz by as we were talking. The different perceptions of learning can include anything from: "It's okay to not know how to do something, and ask for help," or "You should be able to figure this out on your own." One of those views leads toward effectiveness, the other toward a lot of unnecessary effort.

The cost of any new plateau or milestone is the requirement to do things differently than we are used to. To put it simply, if the rowing student wants to learn quickly and become competent, it demands embracing a perception of learning something new that holds to the view: "Maybe I can figure this out on my own and eventually get it, but I will risk holding on to an uncomfortable new view that someone can give me help that will more effectively lead to enjoying this new activity." Frankly, testosterone seems to be an antibody to the willingness to embrace that perception of things sometimes. Unfortunately, those of us with that hormonal inclination, have a difficult time eradicating the myth that perpetuates the perception that: "Men should know how to do whatever is there to do." Women seem more naturally blessed with a willing perception that does not equate self esteem with having to have the answers.

When we begin the discussion of learning the importance of a deliberate shift of the way we look at something, we create another problem. Simply put, it means change. Even the positive process of creating change in how we look at something however, creates stress. It is unfamiliar territory and it is uncomfortable. We're confronted with the stress of another choice, an opportunity to press on or relieve the stress and quit. The failure to acknowledge and accept this, costs us dearly. The tendency to avoid pain and discomfort, whispers a message which suggests that if we were doing the right thing in the right way, it wouldn't be so uncomfortable; therefore, we should stop this nonsense and go back to what was comfortable.

I was talking with a client recently who was dealing with some problems with her son at his school. This bright and precocious child was having any number of different problems in class. Some of his behaviors had alienated him from his peers. His teacher was at her tolerance limit with his constant demands for her attention. I was working with this boy in therapy, and he was making some encouraging progress. However, because of some of his behavioral patterns, he was still struggling with the emotional pain of being aware of people's negative reactions to him.

His mother was both distraught and agitated over the situation. It was understandable to me that she would be concerned, but the intensity of her reaction was curious. As she and I talked about her perceptions of the situation, it became vividly clear that she was invested deeply in some kind of belief about how things should be for her son, and how she should be able to facilitate it for him. As often happens, I made a penetrating comment that burst a dam of emotions. I said to her, "Being a perfect parent will not guarantee a perfect outcome in life for your son." Immediately, the tears flowed, and I could see through her entire body an inner catharsis taking place. It was clear that this emotional reaction was intense enough that I wasn't sure whether she would scream, sob, vomit, assume a fetal position, or just run out of my office.

We had hit a deeply held belief and perception of her role that had let her down. She had years earlier bought a myth. Because of her own unhappiness as a child, she had made a commitment that her children would never have to go through that same kind of pain. The myth that sounded so appealing and gave her hope was: "If you do everything right, your children will never have to suffer and feel the same emotional pain you did."

She was from that point on, however, burdened with the impossible task of being perfect, missing nothing which would put her children at risk, and unfortunately, teaching this particular child that it was up to everyone else, particularly mom, to make his life comfortable. Her primary perception of her son's distress was that it was solely her responsibility to either prevent or resolve. She could "see" no other alternatives.

This woman who is actually a wonderful mother (to a fault), said something profound toward the end of our session. "If I could get rid of this deeply ingrained feeling, it would create an enormous sense of freedom and relief for me." Her perfectionism which had infiltrated every area of her life, was born from a lying myth that engulfed her with a sense that everyone's well being was up to her. While her love and care for her family has to be admired and respected, a distorted perception of her role sabotaged her intent. Her son's life was actually more miserable, because his frame of reference was that there was nothing he could to change things, it was up to mom. By the way, when this family first came to my office, this boy was extremely angry at his mother. The more she tried to make his life comfortable, the more he resented her. What they both didn't understand, is that they were looking to the wrong person to be responsible for how he felt.

The lie of perfectionism is *"You have to be in control of everything, prevent problems, manage your life by getting everything organized, and if you do it well, everything will turn out exactly like you want it to."* Reality on the other hand offers another view: *"Accept what is happening, and learn how to deal with it."*

We're not talking about rolling over in defeat, but just refusing to protest what is going on, and spend what emotional energy we have on trying to figure out solutions and moving toward them. Going on emotional strike is exhausting, and it robs you of using what resources you may already have, and keeps you from finding new ones to resolve whatever is happening. This is the perception that we can do nothing about what is happening. Learning how to develop new deliberate perceptions to manage our experience creates a wonderful opportunity to begin to experience different results. Simply put, this is choosing to look for ways to deal with our circumstances that still allow us to move toward whatever is important that we want to realize. Maybe it means an adjustment of direction, a change of pace ... but never a defeat of the desire.

It always amazes me how in the course of human history and personal experiences, little ever changes. We think the same thoughts, have the same fears, want the same things, and limit ourselves with the same shoot-ourself-in-the-foot pattern. Martin Luther said something to the effect that "I cannot stop a bird from flying over my head, but I can certainly stop it from building a nest in my hair."

We all have arbitrary, random thoughts racing through our minds in response to our experiences and the things we happened to focus on at any given time. The people who are successful in certain areas of their lives, are the ones who are consistent in managing its process. This does not imply the need for constant vigilance, but rather calls for learning new perspectives in the way we look at situations, respond to and feel about our daily encounters.

One critical new way of perceiving things is that there are other ways to perceive things. With all of the people I've talked with in my practice, I can't tell you how many times I've heard someone say, "Oh, I never looked at it that way before," and have that new perception of an experience totally change not only their view, but how they feel ... then how they live.

We live, react and feel according to what we believe or perceive to be true. It is critical for us to learn how to make the distinction between what we believe to be true, and what in reality *is* the truth. It's not what happens to us in life, but what we believe it to be that makes all the difference.

A number of years ago, a friend of mine went through an ugly divorce. His wife left, and with her, much of his earned resources. Because of some of the circumstances surrounding the divorce, his business suffered and did the same shrinking act as his net worth.

Understandably, this successful businessman felt the sting of the personal losses carry over and perpetuate themselves in his career. Because of his personal upheaval he was unable to give the kind of time and interest as he had always given to his business in the past. Consequently, he lost clients, many of the referral sources his business was dependent on, and the growing momentum any business needs to thrive.

The perception he was living with was, "Look at what she has done to me. She's taken most of my resources, she's put my business in the toilet, all that I've worked for is gone, and I'll probably never get back on track again." If all that were true, I'd say he deserved to be depressed and unmotivated.

Then something curious happened. He realized that he had actually been getting tired of his business anyway. The treadmill he had been on had been great for many years, but it was no longer exciting and stimulating. After his legitimate period of whining, moaning, and blaming his ex-wife had passed, he got remarried. Not to a new woman however, but to a completely different perception of what had happened.

In reflecting over the past several years before his divorce, he remembered that he had for sometime wanted to make some professional changes. He didn't in large part due to the difficulty raised by two issues. First, it is tough to make changes in the sources of earning power when you have a lot of fixed obligations; second, his wife had been very insecure about making any changes. As this recall came into clear focus, he began to smile. A new liberating perception came crashing in; his ex had done him a great favor! Certainly without intention, she had given him the circumstances which sent all of the fixed patterns into a tailspin. Everything was changed. What a better time to redirect things.

Everything was a mess anyway — why not?

He went on to start a couple of new ventures which are now not only outproducing what he had done before, but he has managed to create also more freedom with his time and is energized with the joy of rediscovering his creativity. This is not to say that divorce is good, his ex-wife was bad, or that he was a hapless victim. It is rather a willingness and a determination to look at an experience in a way in which you can be free from its negative potential. It is to find a way to look at what is happening that keeps the power of the situation in your court, to manage your consequences.

The perceived reality had been: "I'm toast." The truth however was expressed in a new choice of view: "I have a wonderful opportunity to take all of the scattered pieces of my life and rearrange them in a way that works better for me now."

We will pursue this theme in more detail later on in the book, but it bears mention now, as we begin to build the foundation for developing easier and more effective ways of managing the process of getting from point A to point B.

I have learned a lot from the benefit of being in clinical practice. One of the central themes for those of us in distress is in sorting out the differences between actual reality and perceived reality. Happily we can learn to get out from underneath the unnecessary burden of living out those misperceived and untrue realities about ourselves, our circumstances and those around us. Beyond that, we will learn how to create useful perceptions to look at whatever takes place to give us power over the degree of effectiveness we experience during the process.

Several years ago a great little book was published by two psychotherapists titled *Telling Yourself the Truth*. It was a particularly insightful handbook which I shared with many clients who were trying to sort out their perspectives of themselves and every facet of their lives—from marriage to children to careers. (I recommend reading the book). One of the most helpful pieces of information the authors relayed was simply this: "We often inadvertently tell ourselves things that are not true." The sad outcome is that we act on those thoughts and perceptions, which create results in our lives that are inconsistent with what we really want to achieve.

Unfortunately, we tend to accept false or distorted perspectives about the events and circumstances we experience because they are familiar scenes to us. The outcome of those habitual perceptions can result in anything from the tragic to the confused. Consequently, our views become the cornerstone of collecting evidence (attaching meaning to our experiences) which serves to validate our beliefs.

I once had a female client who complained that men never showed any interest in her. The truth in fact was that she rarely if ever was asked out, and consequently had what appeared to be good reason to believe that there was something wrong with her to make her so undesirable. The facts of her situation were interesting. She worked for a company that sold building supplies. She was at the front desk, where everyday literally dozens of men appeared to order and pickup materials for various construction jobs. Unfortunately, this situation became to her a daily experience of agony, confirming the hopelessness of her desire to have a good relationship with someone. Every customer became to her a further indication that she was uninteresting, unattractive and unworthy of any kind of interest.

As we talked it was clear that these perceptions of herself preceded the experience she was having at her present place of employment. That view of herself as unattractive and unappealing, dictated the way she carried herself at her place of work. Given what she had come to believe about herself through the way she looked at her previous experiences with men, she had developed a predictable pattern of response to the men she met.

As men approached her desk, she would not make eye contact, kept her head buried in the work she was doing while she talked to them, and then sent them on their way with body language which clearly said: "Don't even think about trying to make conversation with me!" The confusion she carried in her perceptions of herself, made the men she had contact with leave puzzled, wondering what her problem was.

It would have been useless to try to give this woman some help with relational skills, better communication techniques, or any other means of teaching her how to better interact with men. The truth is she could have committed herself to develop new tools to try to accomplish what she wanted, but the perceptions she carried of herself would have always been in a state of tug of war with what she was trying to accomplish. Human nature being what it is, we generally stick with what is the most familiar and less stressful — in this case it was easier to operate with her perceptions of herself as undesirable, rather than experience the discomfort of trying to see herself as appealing, and to use new tools to interact with the men she wanted to meet. The perceptions and the goals were mutually exclusive.

The good news to this story is that this woman *really* wanted things to change. We started by dismantling the perceptual system she had built of herself and the mountain of "evidence" she had collected to support those views. She then learned what for her at that time were really arbitrary new perceptions of herself. This at a most basic level meant a willingness, a choice, to look at herself differently. It then meant for her to give herself permission to act accordingly. It all started with her looking at her own eyes.

All she really could accept to start with was that she had pretty eyes. She gave herself permission to let her eyes take the first step in creating change in her life. She let her eyes be the part that she would let people see to begin with.

As trite as this may sound to someone with a strong ego and clear sense of self, this became a simple starting point for a woman, who over the next twelve months created enormous change for herself. She met someone and months later they married. Within a year she and her new spouse started a business. Today, several years later, they own several locations where their business prospers. She did all of this because of two choices. One was to recognize and let go of perceptions that were not letting her have what she wanted. The second was to take a chance on a new way of looking at herself.

Once that decision is made about what we perceive things to be, we begin to watch for additional supporting evidence—even in an unrelated area—and start building a storehouse of what slowly, but surely, becomes irrefutable.

This same principle applies to virtually any situation. A patient in a hospital bed recovering from major surgery is waiting to see his surgeon to find out how things went. The surgeon walks by the room, doesn't come in, talks in muted tones to the nurse in the hallway, then finally walks in looking somber. The surgeon reports that all went as planned but says little more that inspires optimism before abruptly leaving the room.

Relief or concern can come from this encounter. Relief for no bad news, concern for no encouragement.

Of course, things are not so simplistic as this example but the point remains ...that experiences lead to choices ... of which thoughts we will listen to ...

Which lead to perspectives ...

Which become suspected truth ...

Which look for supporting evidence ...

Which then become irrefutable truth in the subconscious ...

In which we become deeply invested. We then live out the demands of those perceptions.

Perception is the major key of managing the events in our lives, and has a phenomenal impact on the eventual outcome of the kind of life we lead. How we look at things and what we believe about what we see becomes the catalyst to the outcome. The way we look at what happens to us in life shapes our daily experiences with our health, in business activities, in competition, in personal relationships—with virtually anything we touch.

I was raised in a typical white, Anglo-Saxon, blue collar, Protestant (fundamentalist) family. After my sorting out of values, views, beliefs and choices, as an adult I knew that my heritage had given me a lot. I grew up in a small community, experiences were limited to a narrow sphere of influence which resulted in fewer, but memorable happenings which left a lasting mark on me. Issues of faith and values were presented in a rigid and legalistic manner. The unfortunate implied message was, "There is only one way to see things." The result is always bias and unintended prejudice that cannot hear pr "see" that there may be another perspective of worth. It makes the necessary skill for effective living, *listening,* an unused function. Some of these values, however, have stood the test of time but have been gentled and softened by a broader view of life and reality.

The central theme in developing healthy and functional perspectives echoes from one of those values: *"You will know the truth and the truth will make you free."* If truth indeed is freedom, then the opposite must be true as well: a false perspective or belief leads to bondage, limitation and inhibition. It amazes me that we are far more inclined to believe that which we are afraid of may be true than to take a risk of believing something more consistent with being healthy, happy and fulfilled. Someone created an acronym with the initials: F.E.A.R. which stand for False Evidence (which) Appears Real. The trick is to learn how in our daily experience to distinguish between perceived reality, potential reality and actual reality.

The objective is to learn how to recognize the kinds of perceptions we're developing about our experiences and how to deliberately embrace perceptions and views which are consistently directing us toward our goals.

This raises an interesting issue however. In spite of the benefits of shifting perceptions to something that creates the freedom to make progress, any kind of change is stressful. The degree of stress is relative to the distance between old and new perceptions a person is formulating. Without being aware of it, an individual in change is calculating the likely outcome of this new experience, measuring the cost to himself, and deciding whether or not it is worth the effort.

A wonderful family I worked with demonstrated all of these signs. The well-educated and successful parents brought their preadolescent son in for an assessment. He was an obviously bright, energetic, articulate and precocious child. Some of his problems included less than stellar academic achievement, poor social skills with his peers, and a very strong-willed personality which had become increasingly difficult to manage. These very capable and motivated parents were at their wits end about what to do for the child they loved, but was absolutely driving them crazy.

Following the assessment, I began treating the boy for the problems he experienced. I worked with the parents to develop strategies of managing his behavior and the responses he was pulling from them. In their typical fashion, the parents worked in earnest with great hope about what changes they might be able to help support. As we began the process, I gave what is a standard spiel about the process of change and expected reactions. As is often the case, their urgency and inspiration left them a bit deaf to that part of the information.

The next time I saw them about a week into the process, they both looked awful. Perhaps lost and overwhelmed would be more descriptive. To my question: "Well, how are things going?" I received several minutes of rapid-fire and confused reporting of the preceding week. "Things are terrible! We thought he was hard to manage before — now we have what feels like a constant state of all out war." In my most practiced caring counselor voice, I calmly said: "Well, that's good. It sounds like we're making great progress." After a few seconds of incredulous stares and rapid eye blinking they responded with "What on earth are you talking about?"

All of the increased verbal and behavioral problems with their son were actually measurable indicators of their success. They had effectively destabilized an unhealthy situation. It certainly felt to them that the stress level had increased, their hope level had decreased, and that things had simply deteriorated.

For me to affirm the apparent worsening of the situation as a necessary and positive indicator arrested their fear and discouragement; because it was an alternative perception of the situation. The new perception was simply this: "We need to destabilize the existing situation as an important first step to creating positive change."

To hear that alternative and foreign perception is one thing; to accept and act on it took courage and faith. They did. We have watched some exciting change occur. The power structure of the family has shifted to where it belongs. Their son's social interaction has become much more age appropriate. His willingness to negotiate and work with them and they with him has shifted markedly.

What is important to point out is that no one in this picture changed. Their personalities are intact, their desires are the same. Just their way of looking at the situation has changed. This has given each of them the freedom to respond in different ways, and create much more desirable results.

In the helping professions, we can easily get the cart before the horse. It is important that we equip people with problem-solving tools, and the learned ability to manage their lives differently. If however, we never change the perceptions, the way we look at things, it really matters very little if we have the right tool. The outcome will simply not change significantly. This is why people say: "Well, I tried that, and it didn't work." Trying harder, doing things differently, or even using new tools is rarely enough to change results of situations we look at in a particular way.

It is not uncommon that the stress of a destabilized view of one's self, a change in academic experience, a change in a family structure, becomes so uncomfortable that a person regresses to the point of origin or beyond and progress comes to a halt. It is for the same reason that an individual who has lost a lot of weight quickly regains the pounds he so painfully shed—the new world the dieter has created for himself is too unfamiliar unless a new perception is attached to the experience that can value the process. The fact that the original state was uncomfortable or unproductive becomes irrelevant. It is a new environment with new values, different language, new perspectives, different food choices and uncertain outcomes. The worry of "can I keep this up?" persists.

Recently I was having what started to be a casual conversation with a professional who was doing some work for me on a project for my business. Something in our conversation prompted him to surprise me with an interesting comment about this theme. He mentioned that within the last year he had quit smoking — and gained 50 pounds. This delightful person, at five foot six inches tall, with 50 extra pounds said: "If that is what it takes to quit smoking, it is *worth* it!" He had deliberately attached a new perception to the price tag of his choice, a lot of weight for someone of five foot six and chose to value the results of accomplishing something important to him. He followed that up with another choice as well — to systematically work to lose the weight — and has lost 15 pounds so far.

If we believe the discomfort of change to be greater than a hoped-for outcome, homeostasis takes over. This is the process in which everything returns to its previous condition. Continuing change requires energy, moving against the power of homeostasis. The learned ability to maintain a new focus, a new way of perceiving the stress created by the changes we're experiencing is the only successful anti-homeostasis agent. If we run out of gas, change stops. If we lose focus, we are inevitably drawn back into old familiar patterns of responding, which in turn reinforces the old views about whatever it is that we are trying to manage. That process creates a kind of comfort because it eliminates the stress of experiencing the unfamiliar. The fact that the original state was uncomfortable becomes irrelevant.

This is not a decision which is consciously designed and implemented. It is accomplished by a process of default, homeostasis returns us to familiar territory. This is the result of what Martin Luther referred to as "allowing birds to build a nest in my hair." In other words, we allow unfiltered, unedited thoughts to take charge, suggesting perspectives which seduce us away from what is stirring inside of us to change. The language here is familiar to most of us: "This isn't going to work," "Why am I trying this?" "So and so said this would happen if I tried this," etc.

Although I learned long ago not to take responsibility for people's choices, I get frustrated, even angry at the insidious and corrupting nature of the intangible lie some people buy. It is frustrating to sit on the sideline and watch the corrosive impact of someone's thoughts and perceptions keep him in a vicious unhappy circle of events. This is I believe, the essence of evil—the lie which convincingly distorts what is true. These are the whispered messages of doubt and fear.

The answer is not to eliminate the presence of alternative views, but to develop a filtering mechanism to rescue us from the vulnerability of perceptions that capitalize on fear and the discomfort of change. We also need to learn the toxic nature of some environments, people and relationships. Those will keep drawing us into the world whose views cannot help but to poison hope and discourage inspiration. What the author of the lies fails to tell us is that if we endure the process of change, the new territory eventually becomes familiar with new comfort and ease. We forget that our presently familiar surroundings and experience were once as unfamiliar, intimidating, or fear-inducing as the new challenges facing us at the moment.

Perhaps one of the greatest perpetuators of "perceptual disorders" are toxic environments and toxic people. One definition of this kind of toxicity, is a person or an environment which imposes itself on you with a demand to do and see things its way or risk disapproval or alienation. One part of my life which I thoroughly enjoy is my horses. They provide great relaxation, challenge, and the more esoteric values of staying in touch with a very earthy side of life.

As in many sports, all kinds of people are attracted to them for any number of reasons. Horse people are, however, one of the most passionate groups I know. Everybody has an opinion, it usually differs from the next person, and everybody is absolutely right, which of course make the other person wrong. As you can imagine, this makes for many interesting "conversations."

While differing opinions are healthy and helpful, the attitude behind them can be toxic. In some circles the attitude can be so pervasive, that it causes those involved to be afflicted with self doubt, abdicating their own good ideas, questioning why they are involved, and turning their decision-making process over to the will of the most vocal platform stompers.

This process can take the love that someone has for something and turn it into intimidation or disinterest. Toxicity destroys everything consistent with emotional maturity, personal responsibility, dreaming and creating, and anything giving life to the human spirit.

On the other hand, involvement with people and groups who support an individual's goals, encourage searching, respect the process needed to experience an individual journey of discovery, gives tremendous strength and support to those people trying to grow in any area of their lives. It is then *their* goal and pursuit, not the agenda imposed by the perhaps well-intended purveyors of what is right. These are the people and environments you want to pursue if you wish to create surroundings for yourself in which the healthy shifting of perceptions can take place.

By raising our awareness of what goes on in the process of change, growth and progress, we can have a major influence over the outcome, regardless of the specific pursuit or goal. When we learn to consciously manage our thoughts and choices of perspectives, it affects our feelings, our behaviors and the long-term outcome of our goals. Our hope is not directed to what may or may not happen to us, but finds its focus in our learned ability to respond successfully to what life confronts us with. We can direct success to the long-term results in our personal lives, in our relationships and in our career, or whatever is of great importance to us..

As a part of my practice I do a number of presentations to various private and public organizations. I call one of my presentations "Perceptual Disorders." This condition is not a specifically diagnosed disorder in our mental health bible—*The Diagnostic Statistical Manual of Mental Disorders.* It is, however, a label I have created for what I've observed as a central theme in working with clients.

Before I was in private practice, I was invited to establish a counseling center for a large church in Southern California. It was a wonderful opportunity for me to be exposed to a variety of experiences with different clients. Some of my first clients were the members of one of the most dysfunctional families I would ever encounter.

This minority, low-income family not only had the common problems often associated with their racial and economic status, but the members were in a perpetual state of crisis. The three teen-aged daughters were either pregnant or just had given birth to a child. The pre-teen son was getting his start in using drugs. The mother had had five major surgeries in the preceding two years. The father was an alcoholic, frequently unemployed.

Their problems were staggering. The mother, who was the only one trying to do something about their desperate situation, was starting to break down. It was clear from her medical history that her body had started that process a few years earlier.

I spent several weeks with the family trying to do crisis intervention. They all taught me a valuable lesson: I could not measure my success on what they would do with the help that I could give them. During an evening session with the mother, she told me about the argument she and her husband had had the previous evening. Were the implications not so sad, the story would be comical. The argument occurred when husband and wife disagreed violently about: "Why did the kids turn out so bad?" All of their blaming and accusations finally boiled down to one piercing perception the husband blurted out to his wife: "Of course it's your fault that the kids turned out so bad. How could it be my fault? I was never here, I was always out drinking with my buddies!"

It was difficult to have a front row seat to such a clear view of a tragic reality. What was not clear to them was their understanding of the meaning of personal responsibility for their individual choices. This emotional quagmire gripped them as they sank deeper into confusion and failure. Sadly, their disordered perceptions about responsibility kept them there.

A happier story began at a local 7-11 store where I stopped one morning on the way to the office and encountered a former client I hadn't seen for some time. I had worked with her, her husband and the couple's two teen-aged sons. The woman looked awful. Her shoulders drooped, her whole body slouched, her eyes were puffy and had a flat and vacant look. When she saw me she offered her lovely, but now strained smile, and her body language told me she was teetering on the edge of an emotional abyss. Serious family problems had put her back to the wall.

It wasn't long after our meeting that she returned to therapy. This time, however she began the journey that eventually led her to some profound changes. Her perception about herself and her family's future had kept her in a dark cell of despair and futility. She had listened interminably to a self defeating tape playing in her mind which kept saying, "You can't change any of this, You can't get out. You have no alternatives that you can live with." Her faith precluded divorce or suicide, so she had only the perceived option of trying to survive the unsurvivable.

The facts were these: She had left home young and moved to another country. As an innocent and naive Protestant, Caucasian, young woman in a new culture, she became pregnant by a young black man. She gave birth to a male child who she gave up for adoption. She now knew nothing of him. She moved to the United States and got married to a successful business man. She had two sons. She went to church, worked in the family business, played the role of a traditional wife and mother. She was unhappily married to her dry, alcoholic husband who controlled the lives of everyone in the family. She lived with shame. Hers was not the life of one whose Christian moral values she believed she should demonstrate.

Consequently her life was reduced to responding to most situations out of the guilt of her failure, apologizing for her sorry excuse of an existence. Consequently she was terminally accommodating, the classic codependent, taking responsibility for everyone else, their feelings and their behaviors.

The myopic view of her history, forced her to do nothing with her life but give it to the demands and expectations of the people around her.

Her journey brought her to the crossroads of some difficult decisions and choices — and she survived them.

Not long ago I received a call from a distant part of the country where she and her husband now live. To hear this cheerful, enthused, and now very accomplished middle-aged woman describe how pleased she is with her life was a warm reminder of why we are encouraged to "weep with those who weep."

I saw her briefly on her visit to town recently; and I wish I had a picture of her from that 7-11 encounter years ago. Her transformation was phenomenal. She had learned the difference between the truth about herself, her past, her power, her children, her spouse, her God and her life. She systematically discarded the misperception and ejected the destructive, old tapes from her mind. The defeated woman who once dragged herself through the aisles of the convenience store was not the result of her kind of life or her circumstances but was the sum of how she had perceived her situation—frightening, depressing and hopeless—until she changed her perceptions.

The tragic reality is that our perceptions and beliefs, when not based on the truth, become totally debilitating. The quality of our lives is not based on our circumstances or outcome of events, but rather on our ability to deliberately discard old views and beliefs, and with the same deliberation design, write and adopt a new script that points us in the direction of our intent.

There is truth and there are lies about what we see. We can learn to manage our views and make life a lot easier, efficient and enjoyable. This is universal truth; it applies to every aspect of human experience.

From the wisdom of the Old Testament and the psalmist David comes a poignant awareness. Exposed politically about his affair with Bathsheba and his responsibility for her husband's death, he was confronted by one of his advisors. In spite of his deceit and failure to live up to his own values, he responded to the confrontation with integrity. He exclaimed, "God, you want truth in the inward being."

At first glance his response may appear curious. There is no denial, no confession, no rationalization, just a reflection of what his internalized grasp of the big picture had taught him. His *chosen* perception was that being confronted and arrested was in his own best interest. A rather different view to what would today be a protest to the exercise of personal freedom. Knowing the truth about anything is the only vehicle to ultimately being successful at living.

It is clear that when the price tag on the desired outcome of our plans gets a little steep, the-path-of-least-resistance phenomenon kicks in. We settle for less. A voice says: "Hey, you're not going to get what you really want anyway, so go ahead and commit yourself to this convenient alternative. It will make you feel much better about not getting what you really want."

The antithesis of this process is that the truth—about ourselves, our loved ones, our difficult circumstances, the responsibility for our problems and their solutions—leads to freedom. It is in this freedom that we are introduced to the ability to alter, stop or change the internal outcome. This releases us from playing the role of the pitiful victim; it defeats the force of lies and half-true perceptions.

It also jars us into an arena where the lights are turned on to our own self deceit. I was recently watching a special 20/20 program about alcohol abuse on college campuses across the United States. During the interviews with several students, it was clear that most of them believed that drinking was almost necessary to having fun, bringing out their inhibited personalities, making them more interesting and desirable.

A researcher conducted a controlled experiment with a group of about twelve young men and women. The object was to measure their physiological reactions to alcohol, any shifts in attitude after drinking, and the impact on the "fun factor" while having a "party." While not an experiment to exacting research criteria, it did show some interesting results. The "party" started off quietly with limited and somewhat flat social interaction (as stated by members of the group was the case at social functions where no alcohol was served). The researcher then provided beer for them to drink at their leisure. Sure enough, the party warmed up, the "fun factor" escalated, and the predictable began to occur.

One participant said he was starting to get tired as usual; another young woman said she felt okay, but probably wouldn't if she stood up. When asked to do so, she in fact reported that she could feel her legs a little uneasy. The conversation continued with predictable comment about the expected results of drinking together among the researcher and this group, at least until he announced that what they had been drinking was non-alcoholic beer.

Following some silence-shrouded surprise, he made the astute comment that perhaps it was more their perceptions and beliefs than the alcohol that helped them have a good time. Although some degree of agreement was expressed about this non-scientific conclusion, the attitude basically boiled down to, "Well, so what, we just want to drink."

Empirical evidence will never convince anyone who doesn't want to be convinced. It is still amazing to see executives from cigarette companies say things like, "Well, there still is no absolute proof that cigarette smoking causes cancer." My opinion is that we don't or won't change perspectives if we create situations where we can't afford to. In these cases, it would "cost" these people too much, socially, financially, or in some other intangible way, to embrace a new and actual reality.

Psychiatrist and author, Scott Peck, has written two books I greatly appreciate. One is *The Road Less Travelled*, and the other, *The People of the Lie*. In the latter, he discusses the issue of evil. It is interesting how he identifies the process of denial as the core issue which becomes evil. Denial, that hiding place from ourselves and the reality we fear, is evil. It keeps us trapped in the self-defeating things we do and keeps us on the not-so-merry merry-go-round.

This tragic and costly denial leads us to less than living well. Like some of our less favorable monetary investments, we get in so deep that it is extremely difficult to divest ourselves. It is here that the astute financial guide would come to the rescue with the advice: "Cut your losses and run." We have to do this with emotional investments as well. The question: Where to run? is the challenge.

Running to the truth sounds too abstract. Our challenge is to make a commitment to discover the freedom from the viewpoint that limits us. The truth is this: There is another view that will allow us to live more successfully. Accepting that is where the change begins.

## *Summary*

Ask yourself a question, "What do I really believe the direction of my life to be?" Take some time with this question, be scrupulously honest. This is not "What should it be?" nor "What have I hoped it would be." There is at this moment a defined and established direction; we want to first become clear on what that is.

# 2

## *Perceptions For New Directions*

A countermeasure to effective living is an assumption that says: "What I think, feel or believe must be true." It always amazes me to listen to the expression of people's perceptions, and to see how far they are removed from what is actually true. And these are not stupid people. They are educated, insightful, aware, but they manage to radically affect themselves and their circumstances with a view that leaves them going everywhere but forward.

Let me share a simple important conclusion: *Thinking it does not make it real; believing it does not make it true; doubting it does not make it false.*

When we accept every thought, feeling and view of things as absolutely true, the only possible outcome is a chaotic life. When our perceptions are in conflict with reality we eventually experience the inner conflict as well. The net results include disappointment, confusion, frustration, anger, fear — any intense emotion which reflects an unstable inner world. Once an idea is accepted as real and gets translated into a belief, it can produce an emotional commitment to a strong position. Once that happens, feelings about the belief direct our behavior and choices. This is the birthplace of the self fulfilling prophecy. The very things we believe begin to come true.

Look at the husband who observes his wife, fresh from an argument with him, who is now being entertained by their children. What does this picture mean to the husband? There are at least a dozen perceptions he could create. Among them: *She loves the kids more than me.* Or, *the children are more fun to be with than me.* Or, *she is using them to make me jealous.* Or, *I'm a jerk, just look at her getting on with things and I'm still fuming.* The list of potential imagined perceptions goes on and on. The pivotal issues here with the disgruntled husband are twofold: He demonstrates that we all have random thoughts and need to learn how to identify them and choose which ones to embrace. Secondly, his choice will not be based on how he feels, but on what he wants the outcome to be. All of us react this way. All of us create situations.

The central theme in this entire discussion about perceptions revolves around this point. It does no good to discuss the phenomenon of variable and arbitrary perceptions, or even how to change them, unless there is clarity on what we want our own personal outcome to be. In other words, what do I want to accomplish, what kind of person do I want to be, and what kind of outcome do I want to experience?

Which of the perceptions would you choose to create the outcome, a reconnection with your spouse? Which imagined situation would justify remaining angry or frustrated? Which perception would leave you feeling guilty and poorly toward yourself? Would any of the perspectives give you hope?

The question we are addressing here is not "Which thought is true?" for the husband, because his feelings of the moment may not allow him the luxury of a clear answer. Rather, as we consider the whole idea of perception, the focus question should be: "Which thought or perspective will take me away from or closer toward the result I want to experience?"

If we're more concerned about embracing a particular perspective than being focused on a desired outcome, we won't get very far.

Actually, it is more accurate to say that we'll get exactly where that perception will inevitably lead us. If, however, we want to be more deliberate and purposeful in managing our lives, then the question is raised of becoming clear about how we want to live, and what values we want to pursue. In other words, do I want a problem-solving relationship? If so, I will only embrace perspectives that allow this to happen. This choice may mean that I won't allow frustration over conflict to disturb me. That is possible. We are so accustomed to certain emotional reactions, it is difficult to imagine responding in some other way. My focus will be on discovering where my responsibility lies, and what do I need to do or not do to take care of my side of resolving an issue.

On the other hand, if the desired outcome is greater proficiency and technical correctness in a competitive sport, then I can only afford perspectives which keep me moving in that direction. Detours of focus don't destroy the potential for progress, but they certainly slow it down. They carry the risk of keeping a person in an old rut.

For example, I was out rowing one day, and things were not going well. I just couldn't get in sync. My stroke was jumpy, my balance had gone south. In spite of good water conditions, no wind, and generally great weather, I just couldn't get it together. What to do? I quit.

What did that decision mean? Either failure or success. Failure is born from the perspective that says: "You should have pushed through." Success is characterized by the words: "Things aren't in sync today. You're off your stroke. Your rowing is coming along fine. Get back at it tomorrow. Go do something else that will work today."

Recovering from physical injury or a health risk presents its own challenges. A necessary question to ask yourself is: "Do I want to recover fully from my injury or illness?" If your answer to the question is a determined "yes!" as distinguished from an obligatory, "I guess so", then you will learn to filter out thoughts and perspectives, whether yours or somebody else's, and tenaciously embrace pictures and images of a fully functioning body.

I am blessed to have a mother of Dutch extraction whose determination and never-say-die attitude is an inspiration. Over the years she has had her share of health problems. A bout with cancer and three hip replacement surgeries among them. As strange as it sounds, I remember very little about her episode with cancer. Her indomitable strength and positive outlook gave no room for not recovering. I wish she would have shared more so we could have been more supportive, but that's how she does things. She is today one of the recovery statistics because of good medical care and an attitude that will not perceive the recovery process as anything but normal and an outcome as alive and well.

Recently she had her third hip replacement surgery. The last one had just not worked and had left her with constant pain and a limp. This one went exceptionally well and she has now fully recovered. True to form, she was on the telephone three hours after surgery, doing all of her exercises as expected the following day, cruising the hospital halls with a walker three days later, and generally refusing to be a victim to the process. She had some normal post-surgery pain, but I had to ask to find out. On one visit to her two days after surgery, the physical therapist came to take her for a therapy session. Seeing me she suggested that she could come back later for my mother, who then replied, "Oh, he'll be leaving soon anyway, I'm ready to go!"

We need to stop and make purposeful decisions about how we want the course of our lives to go. This applies to business, professions, relationships, faith, skills, etc. If we have no focus, we will certainly arrive wherever that directionless condition takes us.

I was recently listening to an excellent tape series in which the author (unknown to me) of *As A Man Thinketh* was quoted. What he had to say applies well to our focus and gives wisdom to all of us thinkers and processors:

> "Man is made or unmade by himself. In the armory of thought he forges the weapons by which he destroys himself. He also fashions the tools with which he builds for himself the heavenly mansions of joy, strength, and peace. By the right choice and true application of thought, man ascends to divine perfection. By the abuse and wrong application of thought, he descends below the level of the beast. Between these two are all of the grades of character, and man is their maker and master. Of all the beautiful truths which pertain to the soul, none is more

gladdening or fruitful of divine promise and confidence than this, that man is the master of thought, the molder of character, and the maker and shaper of condition, environment, and destiny."

In almost two decades and approximately 30,000 hours of clinical practice thus far, I have become a convinced observer of the power of perceptions. If we are to be functional and successful in our humanness, we must be flexible in our perceptions and recognize them as just that— perceptions. This is certainly not to advocate a lifestyle of uncertainty, indecisiveness, of a lack of clarity in our thinking or views. We can become so "open-minded" that our brains fall out—that is we stop using some basic judgment and common sense. Therapists are known to fall victim to this process by trying to not be directive, instructive or decisive about a given situation. Nor do I want to see us limiting ourselves by rigid, accusing and self-defeating views. As always, our search for balance must apply itself here as well.

I've watched sadly as many people pick their perceptions based on familiarity. To perceive our experiences the same old way is probably not too stressful, after all, we are so accustomed to it. In fact a client I saw recently illustrates this point with moving clarity. This young woman is in the middle of a crisis which leaves no area of her life untouched. On top of her personal problems, her mother, probably the only stable person in her life, has been diagnosed as terminally ill with cancer and has only a few weeks to live.

Desperately trying to hang on to some kind of hope, and the progress she has made in therapy to stabilize her life, this young woman was trying to manage her grief with a focus on what will be best for her mother. It wasn't working. She was emotionally overloaded.

During a session, it became clear that she was at a breaking point. After having helped her to relax and focus on some alternative views, her whole emotional state at that time changed dramatically. A few minutes later she reflected about her different feelings: "This is so weird!" The truth was that her normal state had been chaotic and filled with enormous stress for such a long time that a state of peace and focus was totally foreign. I capitalized on the opportunity to say, "No — this is normal, what you're used to is weird."

I watched her face go from confusion, to a wide-eyed, "Oh, my gosh!" as she was shocked into the reality of how she had perceived normalcy. As she sat embracing this new and unused perspective, I watched with great satisfaction the cautiously emerging smile. Afraid to trust, but more afraid to stay entombed in her old world, she took an enlightened step toward a decision she had made weeks earlier. That was to risk finding out if there was a better way for her to live through this crisis.

Seldom is the picture as poignant as with that young woman. It is not unusual though that there is some level of catharsis for everyone who wants to change. The fact that I am sharing with you illustrations from my private therapy sessions should not render those points inapplicable to all pursuits involving change of perspective. To decide to become more effective means the recreation of internal pictures and tapes. To commit to a new direction or goal, carries with it the stress of resistance to change. To know this, regardless of where it's applied, creates the foundation for successful living.

A successful businessman friend of mine has shared some valuable insights with me. By his own admission he had developed a twofold reputation. He was known to be among the best in his field as a specialist working on premier European automobiles; he could also be very difficult to deal with. He shared a few stories, now hilarious, about throwing people out of his place of business in episodes of frustration. To his credit, he took the time to learn better ways of dealing with people in that setting, and has been very successful at it.

His historical perceptions were found to be a major root of the problem. Because he is involved in an industry known at times for its shiesters and con artists, he as the consummate professional in his field, would be outraged to be treated by a customer like someone who was less than professional. I'm oversimplifying the point, but if a customer questioned him or challenged his diagnosis of a car problem, he would perceive it as a condescending insult presuming negatively on his credibility and professionalism. If that were true, anger is at least an understandable response. If not true, as it probably was often not, it created unnecessary conflict.

Realizing that this was not working to serve his overall desires for his business, he went to work on it. He got clear on the outcome he wanted: professional service, professionalism in business, happy customers. He has since chosen to embrace perceptions of customer's reaction, questions and attitudes in ways that allow him to respond in ways to serve his own ends. For example, he has created a model for his business that eliminates much of the problem by allowing the burden of responsibility for choices with the customer. Rather than presenting a customer with a large bill for services performed and having to deal with their shock, questions and challenges to his integrity, he has taken another successful approach.

When a customer presents his vehicle for service and describes its symptoms, unless it is a clear and obvious problem, which on the class of automobiles he is working on, it is usually not, he uses the following strategy. He presents the customer the opportunity to have diagnostic work done, X number of hours at X price. The customer either agrees or disagrees as an initial step. Should the customer opt for this step, once that data is collected, the customer gets a call reporting on the results. At that point the person is told of the work which needs to be done to solve the problem, and the exact price of each part, and the cost involved for the recommended service. It is then the customer's choice to do any or all of the work. No surprises, no misplaced power over one person's integrity or the other person's wallet.

I respect the approach he takes. I'm one of his customers. When I call him about a car problem, I know several things are going to happen. All of them are the result of his choice to perceive the entire process in a way to create the desired outcome, a satisfied customer. He has educated me and his other customers to help him do his job better, recording symptoms, when they occur, how long they last, and under what circumstances they take place. He never says: "Oh, it's probably this." No promises, no pontification, just the facts to start with. Honestly, sometimes I wish I could get a quick answer. I'm sure other of his customers do as well.

What also predictably happens is that when I get a call after his diagnosis, I am given complete freedom to choose what if anything to do. No debates, no need to defend anything on either side. Just gracious professionalism born out of his perception that he is indeed a consummate professional. The customer needs to make his own choice, and if he is asked to do any or all of the job, it will be done absolutely right. My car even comes back washed and vacuumed from an oil change!

His shift in perception from an often adversarial view of customer interaction, to a posture which refuses to allow any internal thought messages implying challenge or mistrust of him and his work, now allows him to interact with even the most difficult customers differently. This change could not have occurred and sustained itself, just based on trying to establish better customer relations. It couldn't have lasted with the internal locomotive of frustration being powered by perceptions inconsistent with good customer relations. As in so many of the cases we will look at, a person's success and effectiveness is more affected by attitudes and perceptions, than technical skill or ability in one's profession. The point is that changing perceptions is an invaluable tool to create change in our reactions and feelings, but we must first get clear on what we really want the big picture outcome to be.

The problem is that we are all already living out our big picture outcomes at this exact moment. The way we feel, react, interact and go about things is based on what we have subconsciously decided is true.

There is a powerful lesson we can learn from a fifteen-year-old boy who came to see me. This good-looking, likable and charming young man presented himself well on the surface, but underneath the engaging facade was the self esteem of a slug. He was from a caring and healthy family. He was raised with good values and was provided with many opportunities. As we got acquainted it was clear that he thought of himself as stupid, unattractive, socially incompetent, with a limited career potential. As I got to know him better it became apparent that actually he was quite bright and capable of success in his life. Ironically he was accomplished in a number of areas. He had a huge "perceptual impairment" of himself.

One day we wandered into the subject of his future, career and dreams. He responded with great sighing, and resigned despair, relating that he was likely to be stuck in a job usually reserved for the stupid and strong. When I asked him what he really wanted to do with his life, I was completely unprepared for the response I received. He immediately transformed into a frightening Stephen King-like character, his eyes squinted with intensity and rage, his jaw clenched, his fists tightened, and his body became rigid. In a robotic manner, he slowly turned his head toward me, and fixed me with an icy stare. His body language was clear. It said: "You s.o.b., how dare you taunt me with the idea that I might be valuable and have a future especially from what I know are totally unrealistic dreams for myself!"

Whew!

We sat in silence for quite a while. He had acted out something that he couldn't articulate—life for him was thoroughly devoid of hope. Anyone who would even hint to him of a different outcome was automatically his enemy, pushing his face into the hopelessness of his perception of himself. Eventually, as we worked together over the next several months, we were able to dismantle one of the most deeply entrenched "perceptual disorders" I've ever seen.

How did I treat him? I let him experience the difference between his perspective of himself and mine. When he made a self-effacing comment, I'd say, "That's strange, I'm confused. I hear you talking about yourself this way, but I don't see you that way. Oh well, you're probably right."

I just let him hang on my pondering. The next time the theme came up— same script, but with one more line: "Well, if you're ever interested in how I see you, I'll let you know, but you'll have to ask." I call this being confusingly confrontive, to destabilize the perspective. It was a strategy to raise the boy's growing curiosity and creeping hope about the existence of another, perhaps more valid perspective. Did he buy? It took six months, but yes!

It was satisfying to watch the transition take place in the young man. It occurred because he traded in an old perspective. Why was he so invested in the idea that he was a failure? He was scared to death that if he let himself hope to accomplish something he valued in his life, he would discover the "truth" of his stupidity and incompetence. He couldn't afford to risk verification of his worst fears. The truth is that perceptions, more than reality, have life-arresting power.

An underlying hypothesis I work with in my practice is that all behavioral and perceptual patterns, even the negative ones, have value. For example, a client may come in and say, "I'm depressed because I can't seem to get my life on track and going in the direction that I really want."

As we investigate background, it becomes apparent that depression is a secondary issue, that it is a response to "the core issue," which, let's say is guilt. Guilt over past failures, mistakes, or misjudgments. I'll often ask such a client what may seem to be a bizarre question: "What are the benefits of feeling so guilty?" As you may suspect, the answer I get is usually surprise and confusion. Remember, confusion confronts perspectives, and unsettles or destabilizes them. The client may express his surprise with something like: "Are you crazy? I'm miserable. How on earth can there be value in feeling guilty?"

Guilt can make wonderful, although complicated sense. If a person does not want to fail again, guilt can be an extremely effective "friend." It will restrain forward movement, insure that no opportunity will be created in which to fail again, and simply keep a person insulated from the risk of a repeat debacle. Fear can accomplish the same thing; so can depression. These feelings and emotions are often responses of choice—usually not conscious and deliberate. Such emotional states become familiar and more "comfortable" than unfamiliar choices which would stimulate more freedom and hope. Following the death of his young son Willie, Abraham Lincoln was quoted as saying: "I believe it is the inalienable right of all mankind to be happy or miserable — I choose the former."

Is limiting ourselves more comfortable or beneficial than pushing ourselves? It all depends on how you see it. The unconsciously perceived outcome of either choice will be the determining factor.

Another client was in the middle of a career transition. She had left an administrative position and was developing a plan to go into business for herself. One day in my office she said, "I don't know why, but I just can't seem to get going and make some of the calls I need to make to get this business going." My often frustrating-to-my-clients question, "What is the value in not doing it?" was met with the typical, "Well, absolutely nothing of course!" As we began to talk however, an issue began to surface. In this woman's last business venture she had poured body and soul into what she was doing, and developed a successful day-care program. Through a series of events due to the political structure of the parent organization for this venture, she ran into a number of insurmountable obstacles. The end result was her withdrawal from the business with a great sense of failure.

For her to now begin a new venture, resurrected an old voice of fear. This voice reminded her of what had happened, how awful it had been, and how she had vowed to never get into a situation like that again. Bingo! A wonderful reason to not make phone calls to get a new business on its way, when the possibility of failure was again present. What this perception was missing was that she and she alone had created something successful before, and events outside of her control had created the problems.

A perception which would allow her to get on with it is more like: "Of course there is risk. The point is to not let that detour you, but to rather develop tools to manage the risks, solve the problems, and change the outcome." Her only failure previously, was being ill equipped to manage and solve the problems which surfaced. The new perception must also be: "This history says nothing of me." That is "I am not defined by the events, I will define them in a way that not only allows me to get moving again, but to accomplish and create what I really want."

The point I mentioned earlier about clear outcomes applies here again. If a person is not resolved to a commitment to go in a new direction, to be focused on a new outcome, there is no need to alter the perceptions to process what is taking place in day to day experience. It takes acknowledgement of a goal, the willingness to take the risks involved in proceeding toward that goal, and being uncomfortable briefly while setting the foundation to establish new perceptions.

Simply put, there is no need to read a road map if there is no clear decision of the destination. You will simply arrive by default wherever you wind up, or run out of gas.

Awareness of the process of perception is the crucial first step in changing the boundaries of feeling and experience in our lives. A person's life need not be in shambles to benefit from this awareness. All of us can improve our ability to live more effectively by understanding and improving our process of building perceptions.

I have a wonderful friendship with a man I met in 1974 at graduate school. We suffered and sweated through a challenging academic environment.

During one of our visits over the past many years he needed a sounding board. He was in the middle of a difficult career transition. Having listened to him quietly until he finished, I made a simple statement of my perspective on his situation and he became quiet and contemplative.

He heaved a big sigh, and sat thinking. Moments later, arousing himself from his introspection, he said: "Okay, I'll receive that." He made an arbitrary decision to embrace a view different from what he himself could see at that moment. It wasn't that what I had said was particularly profound or important. I had simply given him a different point of view for him to consider. His decision involved letting go of a confused and discouraging picture he had created, and made a commitment to use a new view as a new starting place. For him to "receive it" meant that he would arbitrarily reach out and embrace a perception foreign to him, act consistent with it, and with faith, wait for the results to materialize.

Often a different perception is merely reaffirmation of the direction in which we want to continue to move. This keeps our emotional feet on the ground. Our perceptions need to be kept intact so that we can conserve our emotional energy for the problem-solving process, rather than waste it on trying to make a confused view deliver clear and precise results.

One of the tools that can be very helpful to us when we do get seduced into counterproductive perceptions is to recognize the symptoms. They vary from person to person, but we can learn to identify our own and use them as red flag signals to get off of the tread mill as soon as possible. We are all vulnerable to certain circumstances which can consistently get us out of focus. For me two things always do it: 1.) Too little sleep, and 2.) Inattention to good nutrition (i.e., too much coffee, too little good food).

Any number of physiological and emotional signs like walking faster than normal, talking more intensely, increased heart rate, feeling confused, intolerant, unable to concentrate, can be indicators to let us know we're out of focus. Some behaviors are giveaways also: shopping sprees, increased eating, sleeping more or less than usual, becoming indifferent about things we normally care about. When you are able to identify those signs for yourself, let them remind you to not trust the view you have of a specific situation *at that time.* To trust the perceptions born out of stress, confusion, or any destabilized circumstances, is to set in motion a process of inadvertently establishing beliefs about things which lead us in directions away from what we really want.

This by no means implies that we are not able to exercise good judgement. It means that we exercise good judgement by being able to know when we're able to do it, when it is difficult, and the things that prevent it. People who are on the edge of financial ruin exercise good judgement by seeking the services of a good financial consultant to help them manage the crisis. The fact that they got themselves into that condition is irrelevant for the moment — they're now doing something about it.

Seeking out professional help and consultation in any area is simply saying, "I am willing to recognize my limits." That doesn't mean we then blindly turn over control of our situation to someone else, but that we recognize the need for more information, get it, digest it, decide what to do, and take responsibility for the results.

## *Summary*

If you could create a picture that would include all of the pieces of what you would consider a more successful life than you presently experience, what would that picture include that is not a present reality for you? Take some time to look at not only the circumstances of that picture, but imagine as well the daily activities, Write out a schedule for a day in the seek of that life.

# 3

## *Choosing The View That Creates The Outcomes*

O f all of the clinical skills and tools I have acquired over the years, one simple little formula has proven itself to be of enormous value. It has helped me to understand what goes on in my mind and in the development of my perceptions. It works like a light switch to illuminate the numerous potential outcomes of events and experiences in which we become involved.

The benefit of this formula is that it gives us a tool by which we can learn to control our interpretation of events that happen to us. It then becomes unnecessary to spend emotional energy in dealing with "Why is this happening?"

A number of years ago, Albert Ellis developed what has come to be called, Rational Emotive Therapy. One of the primary and most pivotal themes revolves around his simple formula A+B=C. Each of the letters represent a part of a formula which when completed, gives great insight into the question I posed earlier: "Why do different people going through such similar or identical circumstances, come through it with such different effects?."

Each component of the formula gives us the important foundation with which to fulfill the aim of this book. The "A" in the formula represents what is called the "Activating Event." This can be anything from the coffee pot not turning itself on in the morning, to the wrong meal being served us in the restaurant, to an anonymous gift, to an exceptional performance, to a surprisingly friendly response from someone unexpected, to a new physical sensation. These are events and experiences, either familiar, new, unexpected, feared, hoped-for, sought-after, or avoided. Of themselves, they are innocuous, innocent and without any meaning. They are open to interpretation. This then becomes the root of the consideration that *all* events and encounters in the human experience only take on meaning through whatever perceptual view is taken of them.

The added-in component to the formula is "B," representing the "Belief" about the event itself. For the moment we'll skip "B" and come back to it later.

The net result of the addition of these first two components is found in "C," or the "Consequences." Consequences are often seen as the inevitable result of situations, experiences, or events of which we are a participant. Were this true, we would need to discard the formula mentioned, and substitute the equation "A=C" (Activating event equals Consequences). In other words, certain events and experiences automatically lead to predictable results. Or to approach it from another angle, you are feeling or experiencing this because of what has taken place. One is the direct correlation of the other.

Frequently a client will say to me, "I am feeling depressed because my spouse, child, boss, did this terrible thing to me." Or something like: "I am so guilty because of what I did, or so mad at myself because of what I didn't accomplish." These reactions reflect a vulnerability to the actions of another person, the inability to have control over the impact of an event, or the embracing of a feeling that limits any movement. I've heard competitors say things like "I just know this isn't going to be my day today because…" Or a patient in recovery from an illness or injury who says, "It will be months before I can do (a certain activity), because…"

The relative truth of any of these situations is really quite unimportant. I'm not talking about the fact that a situation may in fact have a real impact. I'm talking about doing something about it. The formula will not only let us see what is really going on, but can give us the opportunity to do something other than remain a hapless victim or pawn in events. We cannot control events any more than the weather. We can, however, learn to control the meanings, perceptions and beliefs about them in ways that have absolutely profound potential for change. At the very least, we can affect the degree to which an event impacts our lives.

Back to the "B" part of our formula. Let's visit the patient in the hospital who has just gone through major surgery, and tune in on what's happening. We're looking at the "Belief" process. Understandably, as a person enters the recovery stage of a medical crisis, there are many unknowns. "Will I hurt much? How long? Can I have visitors? Was the procedure a success? Is my doctor happy with the outcome? What do the nurses seem to think? How long will I be here? Will I have limitations? Permanent or short term?"

As is often the case, medical professionals are understandably reluctant to give any definitive answers to these important-to-us questions. Because uncertainty and ambiguity are unpleasant states to be in, we try on our own to ferret out answers. And, because asking direct questions may be too uncomfortable, fearful, or unproductive, we begin to "read" the perceived messages around us.

For example, "Oh, oh, the nurse didn't make eye contact with me this morning. What does she know that I don't?" Or, "The night nursing staff woke me up every hour last night; what are they worried about?"

Any number of observations or perceptions about what is or is not said become fruitful ground for beliefs to become established. Enter the surgeon on his or her rounds. A face of sobriety, cheer, distance, or empathy means any number of things. Let's look at the cheerful greeting for example: It could mean he is glad to see the patient, happy about the success of the procedure, hiding his concern behind a smile, trying to cheer you up before the bad news, insensitive to your pain, trying to impress the attractive patient in the next bed, just being plastic—who knows?

The point to be made here is to acknowledge that there are any number of sides to the chosen expression of the surgeon. First, it is his responsibility to communicate clearly to the patient. Secondly, it is the responsibility of the patient to make a decision about the surgeon's meaning, *and* how he will let it impact him. The propensity to choose one meaning over the other is an important point of focus. Setting aside for a moment the need for clear communication from the medical professionals involved in this person's care, it is ultimately the sole responsibility of the person in the hospital bed to participate in his own recovery by the way he will choose to look at the situation. If the patient wants to get better, it is up to him to make that decision, and filter the experiences he has even with uncommunicative and unfriendly medical staff. The outcome based decision (C) is: I want to recover as fully and as quickly as I can; therefore, I must look at this situation (A) in a way to let me believe (B) that I am going to be successful in my recovery. So, I cannot let the demeanor of my physician, the attitude of my nurse, or the dictates of my insurance company determine what the outcome will be, medically or emotionally. I will need to filter anything and everything from my focus that will give me reason to believe anything other than what I am going to accomplish.

How a person looks at things is certainly affected by his experiences, needs, fears, hopes and habits. The point I want to emphatically introduce here is that we all have the ability to choose the perspective. Understanding the relevance of this ability is the most important part of the formula to alter and significantly affect the outcome of any situation or goal in our lives. How we CHOOSE to see, makes *all the difference!*

If you have an underlying belief system that continually reinforces the idea that: "I probably will never really be able to live the way I want to," then you are habitually programming yourself to edit out certain opportunities and possibilities in your life. "It won't happen anyway, so why try?" becomes an underlying filter that keeps us from even approaching the next step toward a dream and a realistic outcome. It is here that we are confronted with the value of limited perception.

One's desire not to experience disappointment has the value of prohibiting the approach to risk. If on the other hand, you learn to embrace a different foundational belief— "Anything is possible," you will be able to make different perceptual choices about the events that walk, crash, bless, or invade your life.

Several years ago, I considered buying a new home. I was living in a modest neighborhood, in a remodeled, inviting and comfortable house. Nonetheless, it was time to move up a bit and I located a house I liked. The asking price, however, was too far for me to stretch. Still, I kept driving by the house every week or two and on one visit I noticed that the realtor's sign was gone, replaced with a "For Sale by Owner." Later that day I called.

The owner was asking the same listed price , but as we talked I sensed some flexibility. A week or so later an interesting process of negotiation began. But first I made a decision that in retrospect I could see greatly affected the outcome of the sale. I decided I wanted the house, and there must be a way to accomplish it. Come to find out, the house had been on the market for about eighteen months, and was now vacant. Four different realtors had been involved, all of whom quit. The more I talked with the owner, the more I understood why the house remained unsold. He was one of those personalities that you love to hate. The process of negotiating with him and his never-present wife went on for about six weeks. Many curves, road blocks and landslides later, we finally closed the deal. There were times when he so exasperated me that I wanted to forget the whole thing. The eventual outcome, however, was the result of what our formula demonstrates:

A. (Activating Event): Asking price too high; obnoxious seller.
PLUS
B. (Belief): There is a way to resolve each of the problems.
EQUALS
C. (Consequence): Owning the new home.

If we know the objective or outcome we're hoping to accomplish, then we have only one blank in the formula to fill in, to decide how to look at and manage the situation (or, A + ? = C). We eliminate any perspective which inhibits us from reasonably moving toward the goal. For example, perspectives such as : "He acts this way because he's under the financial pressure of owning two houses." Or, "He's stuck in the middle between his wife's demands and my offer." Or, "He isn't able to see any viable alternatives." All of these are perspectives on the seller's performance which allow us to move ahead in negotiations without getting engaged in his attitude. On the other hand, perspectives like: "He is sure an unreasonable so and so, and he will never budge." Or, "This house isn't worth the hassle," are all potentially accurate perspectives, but will most certainly lead away from what we want "C" in this formula to be—owning this particular home.

By the way, as I indicated, I did buy the house, negotiated a fair price, closed the deal in 28 days after concluding the lengthy negotiations, and presently still live happily in what has become a wonderful home. My retrospective: He was a jerk, hard to deal with, but he did me a favor. Since having purchased the home, a number of people have told me that they had made offers on the house prior to mine. All of them complained that the seller was impossible to deal with. The outcome of this situation, who actually bought the home, was in large part due to how the circumstances and issues at hand were looked at, and consequently dealt with.

Perhaps it would be helpful at this juncture to back up a step and look at the tiers of belief that motivate action. When we talk about the distinct differences between the optimists and pessimists of the world, we're looking at what I would label the core or foundational tier of belief. The second level, that which we're in the middle of discussing in our formula, would be the responsive or injected beliefs. The core beliefs are the reservoir out of which all other beliefs and perspectives come. The deliberate response belief with which we respond to activating events is the secondary tier level.

The first level I would also label: Attitude; the second: Choice. Some people try in earnest to make progress at level two, that is they work sincerely at being more aware, insightful and purposeful with their chosen perspectives or beliefs about their "activating events." Their success may be less than spectacular, and then they wonder what is wrong with them or with their attempt. We must first take care of what is first.

If the belief reservoir is a supply of hope and courage, then chosen perspectives will be woven with the strengthening thread of that hope. If the reservoir is filled with doubt, then the chosen perspectives will be threaded with pessimism. As the heart is filled with conviction and belief the head can only reflect the same. I believe that the heart in this sense is developed by our environment, associations, and the general sense of what our own individual world says to us. If our world insists: "You should learn to be satisfied with what life deals you," there will be a constant tug of war between that orientation and the attempt to make choices to change perceptions and our circumstances.

If we are going to make the important transition from reactive perspectives to deliberate new beliefs, we must also look at our environment. If our support system is an environment which is inclined to support old perceptions, we will stay static. If it supports rather new perspectives more consistent with our new goals, we will maintain a more consistent sense of direction.

I know a woman who was married to an ambitious self-starter. She frequently talked with a number of female friends, many of whose husbands were recently retired. Some of her friends were frustrated with bored, lethargic, hanging-around-the-house husbands. She listened to her friends complain so frequently that she became frustrated with her own husband, saying, "You better not start hanging around my house. All men are terrible to live with when they retire."

She had made an ongoing choice to influence her belief reservoir by exposure to a complaining, nagging, and perceptually limited group of people. The perspective was toxic because it defined ALL men, ALL retired men, ALL of the time.

Whatever stream we allow to flow into our reservoir will over time define it. Sweet people become sour. Sour people become sweet. Choices can be made with regard to this foundational level of belief influence. We are capable of recognizing the phenomenon being addressed here, and making choices and changes to slowly or radically alter the flavoring of a belief pool. *It is virtually impossible to draw life-giving and forward-moving perspectives from a toxic source.* We need to take a good look at our resource, test it, and if necessary make whatever changes needed to allow ourselves to make more productive secondary choices of perspective.

A proverb in the Scriptures says: "A man is known by the kinds of friends he chooses." While we reflect ourselves in those friendship choices, we also become influenced by the attitudes, perspective, values, and general beliefs of those in which we invest our lives. If we expose ourselves on a regular basis to toxic attitudes and perceptions, we'll likely start to reflect the same. If we're participants with people and situations that are healthy in their way of looking at things and dealing with them, we'll likely also reflect that.

This is not to imply an isolationist approach to life, only exposing ourselves to one way of thinking. Rather it is to acknowledge the need to stay balanced, limit toxic exposure, recognize it, and deliberately embrace perceptions and people that are consistent with our personal objectives.

Over the years I have had clients who were part of extremely toxic situations. Some of them were families, or businesses or social groups. With all of the sincerity they had, they worked diligently to make progress, frequently with poor results. It often became crystal clear that they needed to step out of their toxic world if there was to be any hope for lasting change or progress. Many of these people changed jobs, painfully withdrew from family members, left dysfunctional relationships, or moved away to be free from the poisonous impact. I've even had clients go so far as to change their names, not to hide, but to rid themselves of association with former environments that had so significantly defined and controlled them. It is not an overstatement to say that some of these situations were absolutely destructive of any potential for a healthy existence. When we're labeled with a name, title, or affiliation, certain behaviors and perspectives are expected. In the most general sense, we usually fulfill the expectations of our environment.

If we're to create the best chance for ourselves to make progress in any important area in our life, lets first look at the immediate world around us. Make choices to detour some toxic streams away from your reservoir. Dig trenches and canals to it from other sources. But how do we know from where to draw? Look at the quality of results in other people's lives, tap into the same sources. Look at your friends. If we have toxic friends and involvements, they MUST go. Don't be fooled into thinking, "Oh, I can handle them." Poison is poison. I'm not talking about an indiscriminate disposal of friends and relationships with people who don't see things exactly the way we do. But I am suggesting that we look at the degree of exposure to anything toxic. Like radiation, we can handle very small amounts in very limited exposure. Increase either the amount or the exposure and we will experience insidious decline in health. Toxic people and situations are no less impacting. Sometimes they're more dangerous, because of the subtlety of a smile, implied care, and innocent sounding conversation. Being strong and smart has nothing to do with combating toxicity. Strong people die of exposure to toxins.

Several years ago I had made a decision to move my practice to a different setting. The existing practice I joined had a relatively large staff. In it were some owner-partners who directed and oversaw the clinical and administrative functions. The expected outcome of the principals in the practice was that I would become a partner. But I was cautious; I wanted to just "date" for a while before getting "married." Thank God for good choices.

As my relationship with this team and the partners began to gel, it became clear that there were problems with one of the partners. The practice had gone through some upheaval in the preceding year. An outside consultant had been brought in to assess the situation and make some recommendations to smooth things out. One of the partners was clearly identified as the source of the trouble. It was recommended that his role be redefined or he should leave. Unfortunately, the situation had become so toxic, and the system so built around the troublesome partner, that nothing was done. The problems continued and worsened. I thought, the impact on me was minimal, I had chosen to stay in my corner, do my work and minimize my involvement with "Mr. Toxic." After several encounters with this person where I was confronted and accused over pathetic, non-consequential issues, I blew up. Frankly, I was shocked and disappointed at my intense reaction, particularly in view of this pettiness. I realized, however, that I was acting like everyone else in that environment. It was not a pretty picture. I gave notice and shortly thereafter, was gone.

I learned several costly and painful lessons. Number one, I'm human. Number two, we must know ourselves well enough to know when things are affecting us. Number three, trust your gut. Our stomach never lies to us. Number four, the convenience of denial generates interest at an alarming rate. One of the most expensive costs was a friendship. The partner-friend who had invited me into the clinic was so immersed in the toxicity, that it took the near-destruction of his business before he and the other partner were able to eliminate the offending associate and start the difficult processes of saving the business and its reputation.

In contrast, effective living involves creating an environment for ourselves, including both circumstantial and perceptual, that gives us increased odds to create and sustain the change we want. This involves everything from what we read, to what we watch on TV, to how we entertain ourselves, to the friends we invest in. Rather than a carcinogenic stream of toxic influences, we *need* the input of perspectives, beliefs, information, coaching and support that is going to sustain a life in a new arena.

On the subject of primary and secondary beliefs, let me share some personal experience which I believe describes the process well. One of my great passions has for years been flying. I was introduced to it early in life, and it grew into a love of flying and airplanes. I am now a multi-engine, instrument-rated pilot, still enamored with the whole business. I have since owned several airplanes, and for a number of years used one to commute out of state to a satellite office.

Doing that much flying, particularly twelve months of the year in all kinds of weather, does get you thinking of risk. Depending on how you look at risk, flying can be anything from ecstasy to terror. There were often winter mornings I would wake up to the sound of wind, rain, and the fact that I had to fly that day. It would be foolhardy to dismiss the weather and say, "Oh, everything will be fine." It would also be rueful to begin to worry. The reality here is a choice about how to look at risk: manage or avoid. To me risk avoidance imprisons much of the joy life has to offer. Management on the other hand, allows life, with all of its incumbent realities to go forward. Having received a weather briefing, done a preflight on the airplane, filed a flight plan, and now sitting at the end of the runway having just completed the pre-take-off run-up, more choices. Same wind, same rain, same clouds, same possibilities for disaster. Underlying beliefs: I am a good pilot, well trained, current in this aircraft and well prepared. Responsive beliefs: I am therefore capable of managing this flight, given what I know, and to do it safely. Throttles forward. This is risk management.

I once flew with a friend who was quite risk conscious. We were taxiing out in his plane on the ramp at a southern California airport. The air was still, the skies were clear with the exception of a single cloud some twenty miles away in our direction of flight. All was fine until he, the pilot in command, saw the cloud. His facial expression changed, he began mild hyper-ventilation, and he started to taxi erratically, got agitated, started to yell at his wife in the back seat over something trivial, and basically crashed on the ground. He asked me to fly us to our destination, which at that point I was glad to do. What happened? His beliefs, both primary and secondary were challenged. His primary belief was that he was not a particularly good pilot, and that there existed a weather risk. His secondary belief was that he could not manage the situation.

As an outside observer, I realized his original premise was not true. Although he was not instrument rated, he was an entirely adequate private pilot in V.F.R. (Visual Flight Rules) conditions. His frame of reference about weather flying was limited, so he saw *any* weather as beyond his level of risk management. At that moment he was in fact an unsafe pilot, not because of his skills, but because of the out-of-formation thoughts and perceptions in his head. Because of his primary belief, his secondary one was actually true, he couldn't manage the situation. Had his primary belief been in focus, he would have managed the situation just fine. Had he encountered weather along the route beyond his capability of managing, he was more than capable of making a judgment about it and flying to an alternate destination if necessary.

There are other pilots I would never fly with under any circumstances. They are the "No Problem" group. Not only do they not worry about avoiding risk, they give little or no attention to managing it as well. There is a saying in aviation circles: "There are old pilots and bold pilots, but no old bold pilots." Perhaps to translate that into our world of perceptions we might say: We will either choose our perspectives, or be enveloped by those conveniently presenting themselves to us. One or the other WILL happen.

The point to all of this is that we need an anchor, a foundational belief, to build perceptions on that will help us live successfully. It is legitimate to take an arbitrary belief, one that may be totally inconsistent with what we presently believe, and insert it as a new foundation to build from. Let me give you one such belief: "All will be well, regardless of what is happening." *Regardless* says, "I will refuse to give any present power or future hope away to what is staring me in the face." Those things cannot be ignored, and often demand our attention, *but* cannot be used to define the outcome.

A truism that is important to maintaining effective perceptions to manage events is this: "We cannot attach our hope to specific outcomes." If our sense of well being or quality of life is linked to the specific outcome of a situation, we are creating a perception of things that is going to work against all of our energy — there are just sometimes too many variables to preclude an exact outcome to a situation. This doesn't mean we just settle for whatever happens, but that we develop a way of looking at all of the variables, changes and surprises as just that — not indicators that things will not work — but maybe just a little different than originally visualized. Success in anything *cannot* be defined as an exact and complete copy of the original idea. Success, particularly in living, is in maintaining movement, balance, focus and learning to enjoy the outcomes, sometimes full of surprise, and far removed from the original plan. Life is not a blueprint, requiring exacting reproduction of a fixed and unalterable plan.

Our hope can rather be attached to learning the skills of managing situations, being adaptable, resilient, and willing to stay on track to find a way over, under, around, through — some means of maintaining progress and at least having a significant impact on where we finally arrive.

The beginning and end of all of this is a willingness to choose a foundational belief which will allow for this whole process to occur. Living effectively includes getting anything, including ourselves and our beliefs, out of the way so that we can really come to embrace a way of living we each hope to realize. *It can happen!*

## *Summary*

Select a new belief to insert in response to situations that occur in one area of your life that would give you an entirely different way to see the situation. Use that new perspective consistently for 30 days — see what happens

# 4

# *Winning At Making Failure Unnecessary*

Several years ago in the Los Angeles School District, a deliberately instigated rumble started and caused a significant upset in a certain classroom. It started with a determined high school teacher. The impact this man had on his students was so profound that he received national attention, and a movie based on his story, *Stand and Deliver,* was made. The movie was about the drastic turn-around of students' attitudes and performances in a school which had historically suffered from a poor academic track record.

What is fascinating about this story is how the problem was addressed. The approach used to bring about change was not an attempt to make students learn better or for teachers to teach better, but something much more fundamental was put to work.

This teacher bombarded his students with a new view of themselves. With unrelenting, dogged and persistent confrontation, he created an opportunity for them to see themselves differently. Rather than their persistent beliefs about themselves as people who couldn't benefit from education, he held up another view. He let them see themselves as people for whom an education could make an enormous difference. He presented a new perception of themselves and their potential for the future. They could go to college if they chose to qualify. They could make career opportunities for themselves, and finally they could make of their lives what they wanted. What is important to realize is that this entire process started with the interjection of his view, not the alteration of theirs — that took time.

He refused to accept the perspective that prevailed in the classroom. He took sarcastic, surly, anti-establishment kids with bad attitudes and helped them become highly motivated and accomplished human beings. He challenged the way the kids saw themselves—their perspective. He created a new perceptual opportunity for them to see themselves differently. He made their old view of themselves unnecessary. He proved that the primary and most beneficial way to change is to confront a person's perceptions of himself and his situation. If the individual is open to looking at things differently, the method works. It may take constant focus on the view that was foreign to them as it did in this situation, but it has the power over time to radically change even the most difficult people and their lives.

The historical social structure of these teenagers necessitated conformity. If only one student were to embrace the new perspective and excel in an academic world, the act would place him outside of the norm. The unwritten belief system stated: "To be within the norm is important; to become abnormal, even toward something good is to be totally avoided." The social strata of the kids had little room for the college-bound and profession-seeking mentality. The social dilemma was this: personal development equalled social alienation; social stability equalled personal life long limits. It was therefore *necessary* to maintain the existing perceptions of themselves. Academic-avoidance behavior became a social anchor.

For quite some time, even with encouragement from their dynamic teacher, these kids stubbornly held on to their perceptions of themselves and resisted all alternative views. Their ability to perform scholastic tasks had nothing to do with raw intelligence. Their perceived reality had become self-fulfilling reality, which they demonstrated by unified poor achievement. Ironically, they all actually demonstrated a high level of achievement that was consistent with their cultural world, in this case the goal of resistance to what the school system expected as a means of demonstrating social acceptability. The task was not to push and prod them into doing something incongruent with their cultural norm, but rather to take their present level of commitment and success (avoidance, resistance, and devaluation of education), and redirect it toward something that would serve them better. This is not trying to make losers into winners. It is taking those who are successful winners at a loosing game, and help them become equally successful at a game that will produce better self-serving results. It takes a crusader and a risk taker like this particular teacher to confront deep-seated beliefs. It also takes great wisdom. Deeply held beliefs will not change with confrontation, encouragement or coercion. All efforts, categorically, will fail. There is a singular way to stimulate change. It begins by wisely recognizing the *necessity* of the existing perception. It is followed by strategic steps to make that perception unnecessary. That is the crack in the door to move toward effective living.

The challenge took him immediately outside of the defined boundaries of existing perception and belief. His own beliefs were questioned—the validity of his perceptions, his value as an educator were on the line. He took an unconventional position without any factual or scientific foundation, and went to war over it. Had his self esteem not been superbly intact, his battle most likely would not have started, or run out of steam rather quickly. He had no support and operated strictly from his own unpopular and unfounded stand. His perspective was upheld by nothing more than his strong inner conviction and resources to continue to hammer away at his enormous challenge. And, he won. The terms of success for these kids, losers by some standards, was redefined in a way that they were allowed to *see* for themselves what this new approach could do for them.

Two conflicting issues were at work in this case. One was the surface issue of getting these kids educated, the other represented the social, perceptual and environmental inhibitors to that goal. These distant two poles are reflective of the inner values conflict every person experiences in the face of significant change. If the teacher had focused only on the first issue and tackled the academic problem, he would have failed miserably.

When the teacher focused on the underlying issue, he set the stage for a successful strategy and outcome. To undermine an existing belief one must make it unnecessary and replace it with a new necessary one, and things will change.

This inspired teacher had little if any apparent evidence to support a different perspective for his students, other than his stubborn conviction that they could be better than they thought they were. He didn't ask the kids if his perception was accurate. Nor did he look to their parents for support of his belief. His success was in taking an arbitrary belief, embracing it, making it his own belief, and then acting it out with relentless conviction. He took a perception and accepted the challenge of finding a way to inject it into a group that had no interest in hearing it.

What he did is similar to the process of parenting. With young children, parents serve as conscience, guide, protector and provider. Eventually, the parental role is to completely transfer their parental responsibility to the child. If that doesn't happen, a child never needs to shift focus about who is responsible for what in his life. Had this teacher simply leaned on his students about the value of an education it would have been only someone else's goal for them. He had to find a way to get to the *parent* or *teacher* inside of them. He had to help them see what he did, and believe what he did, which was the value of a good education and that they were worthy of it.

In a way photography can be a lesson in adjusting perspectives. There all kinds of views through the view finder. But I'm not referring to the subject matter, but what happens especially when you view through a telephoto lens. To be able to zoom in and out makes for interesting shifting of perspectives. With the lens adjusted to focus on a near-point subject, things in the distance are obscured or eliminated from view. To zoom out, the scene changes—from one totally different world to another. What was at one moment in the foreground fades and disappears. Things which had not even been visible before, appear. As we continue to adjust the lens, formerly obscure images become crystal clear. We just didn't see them because we didn't have our optical lenses focused in their direction. The same is true of perceptual lenses. Our focus is our reality of the moment. We build life-long patterns from the accumulation of all of those momentary perceptions.

Someone may be pointing something out to us which is within our potential field of view, but if we are locked in on our view or our particular adjustment to the lens, we may be unable to see their point. Being open and ready to accept another view especially when things aren't working for us, becomes an important step to personal growth. We can be so philosophically invested in a perspective that we don't notice when it isn't working. It is the risk of allowing someone else to adjust our lens. Sometimes that requires an invitation.

Several years ago I was working with a firm which was expanding the range of its services. This company was in the business of helping other companies better utilize and take care of their own employees. The management had accurately projected an area of new business services which they could provide in the field of Employee Assistance Programs. The company had a good product, and a quality team of people to do the job well. Over a three-year period they had invested a great deal of the company assets to develop this program to get it up and running.

This new business secured some good contracts with several major companies in their region. The clients were happy with the services. There was, however, a building crisis. Not only were they not generating a positive cash flow from this venture, but it was putting their parent company at risk of going under. In reviewing their situation, several factors became clear. First, their fee structure was built on being competitive, not successful. Second, their overhead was killing them. They had large, beautiful and prestigious offices, cars and equipment. Most of it was unnecessary to their task. Third, they had fallen into the "Rob Peter to pay Paul" trap of financial management. The success of the parent company was used as a cushion to poor management of the new business. Fourth, only one of the owners was really making the decisions. It was clear that he was overly invested in the management of this new venture according to his need to project a particular image of himself and this new company.

Despite all efforts to design a plan to redirect the resources and energy of this company, all efforts were sabotaged by this particular owner. He was so invested in his view, he would not allow for the reality to sink in, that his way of doing things was not working, and things would never turn around without some significant changes. The other owners were so invested in the view that this particular owner was a genius who brought incredible ability to their firm, that they couldn't, or wouldn't see the reality emerging.

The sad and totally unnecessary outcome of this story is that the parent company suffered huge losses. Even though the owners were eventually able to salvage it from ruin, they paid an enormous price. They had all put virtually all of their personal assets on the line, including their homes. The company and its employees suffered, as did their families. All sadly due to the unwillingness of one person to make a simple acknowledgement: "It isn't working." What could have been a very successful venture became an albatross. All because of a stuck view-finder. For this particular firm, the answers to their problems were fairly straightforward. The unwillingness to be open to another perception destroyed any chance of meaningful recovery. The *stuck* perception they were operating with went something like: "If we give up or modify this venture, we will look foolish given all of our investment and our enthusiasm about how well this program is being received." They let what they believed would be the view of outside sources dictate what any action on their part would mean. In contrast, we *must* decide how *we* will define an important decision and action, and act that out regardless of what may be defined from people outside of that situation.

A far more productive perception about making some significant changes would be: "Because we believe so strongly in the viability of this program, we are going to continue an ongoing process of refining how we approach it to make it more successful for our clients and ourselves."

One business consultant I know makes clear her criterion to

work with struggling companies. She insists that before she begins her work, she wants a commitment from the major players. "If it is determined that you are the problem, will you leave if necessary?" It requires a willingness on the part of everyone to do whatever it takes to turn things around.

Another company took an entirely different perceptual view to problem solving. This particular human resources firm was doing extremely well, in both national and international markets. They were growing because of the excellent service to their clients. Their dilemma was dealing with how fast to grow, and how many new clients to accept. Like any company, they were reluctant to turn away business. Their decision reflected a willingness to hear an outside perspective.

Their first concern was, "If we turn away business we will lose that potential customer." The perception they were given as an alternative was: "If you decline their business at this time because you will be unable to serve them with the high degree of attention you give your clients, you will demonstrate a commitment to integrity and quality service. The likelihood is that they will want your services even more, and be back." That is exactly what happened.

What this company did was risk embracing a new perception of their situation, and acting consistent with that view. As they were able to manage their growth and prepare themselves to accept additional business, they did it without the pressure of trying to keep up with increased demands on their time, and worry about providing continued quality service to all their clients.

Of the many things that can alter our focus, environment is a major influence. If the environment presents a problem sometimes the best alternative is to *move* —both physically and emotionally. It may be impossible to see things in a different light from where we are, or with whom we're involved. We need resources to help us move, and then keep moving so that we don't fall back into an old pattern. When we need to make big decisions or sort out big problems, it helps to get in a different environment to think it all through. Our perceptions of things can be so tied to our familiar environment and normal stimuli, that it helps a great deal to do our sorting out in new surroundings. Get out of town, stay in a different environment for a few days. Get away from the normal and familiar which keep us looking at things the same old way. Talk to someone different, coming from a different angle. New perspectives are born only in new environments — sometimes physical, or emotional or circumstantial — or all of these. Find whatever kind of arena change you need to be able to capture a healthier or more productive view.

Once we have a grasp of that new perception of where we are going and how to get there, the next challenge is to keep that view clear. Not only are there distractions and things that confuse what may have been a crystal clear view, but there is a seductive value in those distractions. The value in distraction is in not having to discover what may happen with any new direction. It eliminates the stress of learning to exercise a new perceptual system. We don't have to worry about learning to look at things differently.

One of the most seducing patterns that distorts our focus are all of those good and necessary things we need to take care of in our lives.

Some years ago I had a client who had gone through some major changes, including the loss of his job. He had no clear idea of what to do to get back on track professionally. At a personal level, he had a number of not so unusual demands on his time. His house needed repairs, his children were having problems in school. He had a friend who needed some help. His church was in need of volunteer help. His full-time job became managing all of the good and important things that cried for his help and attention. How can we say "No" to children, friends and God?

These good and noble things became his nemesis. He was seduced with a distorted perception of the valid demands on his time, and had no way to get out from between that rock and hard place. It taught him that: "You must always say *yes* to important things." A healthier perception of the situation does not imply neglect of one's values. I helped him embrace a new perspective. I literally created a schedule for him in which he had "slots" of time available for giving his children homework support, time for his church and work on his house. Those things had to be put in time slots so he could conscientiously manage the rest of his life. He learned to allow himself to be responsive without becoming a captive. That process, while being learned, was *very* uncomfortable, particularly because he had taught the people around him to expect an immediate response to their needs. He had also inadvertently taught them that *he* was the one who was responsible to manage their needs and crisis. He had taken from them the opportunity to develop their skills to manage the things in their lives that they were capable of doing.

Another client was an administrator of a parochial school. She was a highly motivated and capable individual. She worked incredible hours by choice to do an outstanding job. In spite of her efforts, she was about to be fired. Her perspective had been that in order to do a good job she must maintain an open door policy to all of her teachers, support staff and other employees of the school. As good as she was, no one could stand her. She was harsh, quick, controlling and intolerant in her responses. She was mortified at having been referred to me as a condition of keeping her job. This dear lady was lost, depressed and angry.

As we began sorting through the details of the situation, a couple of important things became clear. Her expectations of herself were nothing less than impossible. She was trying to fulfill a mental list of tasks with a management style that was also unrealistic. This lady, who I saw as kind, compassionate and concerned, had made herself difficult to be around because of self imposed pressure. For example, we immediately killed the "open door" policy. What perhaps sounded like a good idea gave her no time. The constant flow of traffic interrupted her incessantly. It kept her from getting things done. Having made commitments and promises to people to get certain work accomplished, she was being prevented from doing these things by an unrealistic availability to everyone. She was creating the pressure for herself which made her sharp and irritable.

The perceptual test was this: "Is it helpful in the big picture to draw boundaries so that I can do my job well?" It also meant that she allowed for her primary belief to be challenged. That is, was she willing to continue to believe that "all things for all people all the time" was really a good foundational belief? This lady became a success story.

She accepted a new position and used different perceptions of her role to develop a different management style. She was effective, not because of using another set of management tools, but because she altered an ineffective belief which produced unworkable perceptions.

Every person has a picture of himself—good, bad or ugly. This picture dictates how we feel about ourselves, act toward others and approach life. The picture is stored in our minds, unseen by most. Few are allowed entrance to this secret, sacred and private arena of thought. Often, we don't know ourselves anymore thoroughly than strangers do.

In order to get acquainted with our inner self we need to ask ourselves the question: "How would I like to see myself?" This is not to be confused with: "Who is the real me?" which represents a left over from the soul-searching theme of the Sixties. That question leads only to a never ending search while trying to define the variables of personality that can constantly shift until an anchor is placed somewhere we want to be — out of choice. Although we all possess our own unique personality traits and talents, the real function of the self can only come to life by taking the risk of deliberately selecting the results we want to realize. The heart can tell us more than the head. The mind wants to analyze, judge and evaluate, which is one way of destroying inspiration, motivation and growth. For example, one of the best ways to kill love and passion, is to try to analyze and explain it.

The heart doesn't debate the dream, but acknowledges it and gives us our starting point. Unfortunately, most of us don't have a clear picture. We know what we do, what we want, and what we like, but the real self often remains a mystery. The "real self" is "the most *want* to be self."

It is this "most *want* to be self," that presents the risk factor. *Can I really be this person? Will I make a fool of myself? Dare I let anyone know this inner secret?*

We're not alone in our world. Those around us believe about us what we let them think we believe about ourselves. We've taught them our perceptions of ourselves by how we behave and what our life choices are up to this point. They have little choice but to believe that what they see must in fact be the real "Me."

This is not at all unlike the problem some professional actors—especially character actors—face in their careers. Because actors like John Wayne were typecast, it was hard to see him playing any another role. Can you imagine the Duke playing a passive, compliant, indecisive geek?

Whom do you think of when someone describes a man in a rumpled rain coat, an unlit cigar dangling from the corner of the mouth and a respectful, well-timed ..."Just one more question, ma'am?" Peter Falk, of course in his role as *Colombo*.

Like the character actors, we too get "type cast" by our environment. People are used to the role we play and can't imagine it changing. To risk revealing our secret and sacred view of *"the desired to be self"* is to risk being criticized. But, we do not have to ask for permission to change. We have to learn to change without paralyzing ourselves with what other people think about us. We have to be behind the camera. We need to move from the role of "type cast" actor to director. To direct the scene is to visualize what we want to see in the last frame of the film, and direct accordingly. There are many talented film makers who both direct and act. I suspect that the directors are motivated by the challenge of controlling the end result of the project, while actors protest the limitations imposed by being only in front of the camera, simply because the director has the greater influence over the final result.

I had a client who was a retired military colonel. He was a highly decorated veteran of several major conflicts, including Viet Nam. He was five years into retirement and in his early fifties. He had several aborted attempts at settling into a new career. To begin with, he broke his own type-casting by coming to my office. For the first time in his life he was lost and had little clear direction. The worst part of it all was his shaken belief in his ability to exercise good judgement and complete a plan of action. He was an absolutely delightful and engaging personality. His appearance was military, but his demeanor and attitude exuded warmth, understanding and a balanced outlook on life. I was aware of my own tendency to pigeon-hole him as a certain type of person, given his background. Basically, that was one of the big struggles he was having in getting resettled in a new career. Everyone seemed to be unable to see him except as a person who had worn a uniform.

He had come to the point of flinching at the idea of thinking about what he wanted to do. His belief system had shifted from conquering objectives to one of expecting regular ambushes. Actually, he had done a good job at selecting different fields of business that interested him. He had effectively interviewed for positions he was eventually offered. The problem was that he was both astute and naive. He was a very bright man and an effective leader. He simply wasn't prepared for the corporate political structure, the petty infighting, and not being insulated by rank — he was bewildered. For those reasons he lost two good positions. I believe these were the first of what he would call significant failures in his life. He was confronted for the first time by an ugly perception of himself. "Maybe I cannot make it in the real world outside of the military structure."

The inner conflict of self perception had him paralyzed. We discovered a couple of interesting things in counseling. This hesitation causing perception was not new. It had confronted him a a child, in the sense of a general concern about doing well in life. This recent bout with perceptual turmoil resurrected those old feelings. His personal life during his military career had some major crises. He had managed those problems and his feelings about himself with his contrasting mastery of the occupational side of his life. However, he was now without that luxury.

We began by acknowledging the bombardment he was under at the time. Old beliefs had been resurrected. "Maybe I can't make a success of myself. I don't know what I should do with my life, and am unsure if I can make a good choice," etc. New perceptions were emerging. He was uncharacteristically in retreat. To simplify things, we put him back in focus. The lens on his view of himself had slipped out of adjustment. As the view of himself clarified, he began to move ahead again. He was industrious, very insightful and intelligent, and his restlessness was a testimony to his unwillingness to accept a mediocre lifestyle and occupation. Getting restarted for him required a jump start — someone from outside of his clouded view of himself to bring it back into perspective for him. Beyond getting a clear view of himself, we got the heart engaged again. Who did he really want to be and what did he really want to do? Gladly, he rose to the occasion. This defeated warrior became again the moved-from-the-heart man with purpose. He eventually selected a career for which he was extremely well suited and began the steps to fulfill it. Two things had changed. First was his renewed willingness to embrace a familiar perception of himself, and take a leap of faith toward it. Second, was a new awareness to consistently filter out the ambushing thoughts that defined this period of understandable adjustment as evidence of incompetence when out of uniform.

To direct yourself you have to look carefully at the role you want to play, write the script, and see to it that the end result represents the dream. What is your "dream" or picture of your *most desired-to-be-self*? Take some time, close your eyes, search your heart, and see the picture appear on the screen of your mind. Don't give the picture away. Don't share the picture with anyone you have not already experienced as capable of giving you realistic and balanced feedback. This is the most delicate stage of creating deliberate change. Once that vision is allowed outside of the sacred inner space of your mind, like a newborn child, it is at immediate risk if not cared for with the protective and nurturing of someone with a reason to keep it alive. It is your script; retain the right to be its sole writer/ director/actor. And by all means, don't call in the critics. Critics belong to the "Why it can't work" crowd.

I love the story of Sylvester Stalone. He rose to fame on the heels of his movie *Rocky*. The film is symbolic of what he went through to get the project into production. Virtually every agent, producer, director, and anyone else who "counted" in the industry turned down the idea for the movie. Stalone risked, and he had to live with the rejections, humiliation, and ongoing disappointment in trying to get his movie produced. After he endured what I understand to be well over 100 rejections of this project, someone finally offered to buy his script, for a reported $150,000. The *rationally minded* of us would assume that an unknown actor who was broke, and had no other viable means of supporting himself and his family would jump at the opportunity to make a respectable amount of money for his script. I am curious about what his outspoken mother told him when she heard he wouldn't sell.

He didn't ask the entertainment industry if his project had worth. He had made that decision himself. He dreamed, he committed, he didn't listen to the voices of *reality* or *informed perceptions*. He had chosen what to he wanted to do. The filters went up, so that he could keep moving.

There is power in staying behind the camera. Take control of the focus of the lens. We can tap into our creative genius. We don't ever want to be typecast into comfortable but eventually unfulfilling roles. It is important not to sabotage that process once it gets started, and to keep the momentum going.

The genesis of effective living is: "Who do I want to be?" Forget the unproductive "Yes but" responses. Fire the critics. Don't ask permission. Just Do It.

Any number of times I have taken virgin flyers up for an introduction to the exhilaration of flight. Many of them have wanted to get a feel for what it is like to actually control a plane. Everybody does the same thing: chase needles. Of all of the instruments on the panel, several give indication of the attitude of the airplane in flight. These gauges tell if we're climbing, descending, turning, and at what rate, etc. My standard instruction to these flying neophytes is "Watch the horizon, stay level with that, and everything else will take care of itself." The truth of this suggestion virtually never gets utilized. Everyone wants to watch the gauges, and invariably starts to *chase* them. Before long we are porpoising our way through the air, creating for ourselves the uneasiness of unusual physical sensations which come with loading and unloading G-forces on the body, disrupting the balancing center of the inner ear, and causing verbal commentary of all sorts, as control is soon less than desired. The way to fly or do anything smoothly and efficiently, is to watch the trends, and only respond to them once it is clearly a trend moving at a rate and to a degree that can actually have something done about. If we allow the perception that fear brings, that everything is going wrong, it soon will be, as we jerk things around to try to create stability.

If we feel the necessity of responding to every change, we become so busy bouncing around, that we cannot see that movement may actually be occurring as we want it to. Three things are good to watch for in measuring change, problem-resolution or progress: Frequency, Intensity and Duration. Each of these important measuring devices give safe, sane and reliable feedback on the real state of affairs in our pursuit. Let's say you've started a new business. The first few weeks and months are spent with energy, excitement and drive toward this new goal. Things start to happen, and the business starts to grow. Three months later, things slow down. What does it mean? It's really simple and clear: "Things have slowed down." Nothing more, nothing less. Period. The question is not, "What does it mean?" but "What will I do?" Getting busy again would be a good start, consulting with someone who is knowledgeable would be another, DON'T talk to those who were concerned from the get-go that it wouldn't work.

Measuring "frequency" means we watch the trends in the frequency of the drops in productivity or progress. If we see a pattern of greater length of time between drops, i.e. less frequency, we're on the right track. If the frequency of drops increases, then look for solutions. The same is true of intensity. If the drop in business volume or progress we're measuring drops from its high point 40 percent the first time, 39 percent the second time, 45 percent the third time, and 20 percent the fourth time, we're probably headed in the right direction, as long as we're seeing a rebound to near the starting point. The intensity is reducing. So also in measuring duration. If each drop starts out lasting five days, but over time begins a recovery at four days, that is significant measurable change.

It would be less than realistic to suggest that these cycles still don't feel good. This is the "Back to Square One" scenario — it feels that way. Our feelings create the perception, which creates the belief, which then stimulates behavior, often unfortunately in the wrong direction. Intimacy or safety is not lost because of disruption — only when movement is not stimulated toward resolution.

An analogy I've used often with people illustrates the point well. Let's say you've decided to take an ocean cruise from Los Angeles to the Hawaiian Islands, a long time on a boat in the middle of a lot of water. Let's say the ship is headed in a westerly direction. One day, mid-ocean, out of visual contact with land, you decide to take an extended walk on deck to enjoy the fresh ocean air. Having walked to the bow, you begin your walk to the stern. Part way toward the tail end of the ship, you stop in utter confusion and panic. Your racing thoughts of anxiety say to you: "Hey dummy, you're going the wrong way! Hawaii is the other way. Turn around and walk in the right direction or you'll never get there!"

The point is simple. As long as you don't jump ship, your original decision and commitment to get on board takes care of the duty to get to your destination. Choices, variables, the uncertainty of momentary actions, and a lack of straining at the bow, staying at the leading edge, are all a part of any journey. The activity on that ship is not stationary. There are many events and happenings, none of which affect the outcome, unless it is believed to be a threat to a safe arrival. Can you imagine the captain continually announcing that all passengers stand facing the direction of travel for the entire duration of the trip?

## *Summary*

How would you describe your "most desired-to-be self?" What would you need to do differently to become that person? The challenge is this: Accept that the picture you visualize of yourself is in fact entirely possible. Then ask yourself: "What will it cost me to become this person, and, what will it cost me if I don't?"

# 5
# *Why We Are Where We Are: Choices That Create A Way Of Living*

While looking at many of the components of creating an effective life, one interesting fact emerges. Over the last many years in practice, I have conducted a number of seminars and conferences. Among them have been several for groups of single young adults. Some of the issues addressed were around relationships, developing life partnerships and emotional maturity. I enjoy saying things in such a way as to get things stirred up a bit, which tends to create a lot of energy and discussion. One of my opening lines for many of these seminars involving decidedly less-than-happy-about-being-single people is "You are exactly where you want to be in your life, right now!"

It was no surprise that this particular comment was met with anything from confused silence to outright vehement protest. How on earth could I be so insensitive to their undesired state of singleness!

Most of us stand somewhat removed from those activities, people and circumstances which we believe would be a more ideal realization of our lives. To allow ourselves the tantalizing luxury of dreaming would often find us with a different job, a different house, a higher income, more freedom, perhaps a different partner, some alteration of our present lifestyle—things which we believe would add a greater level of quality and enjoyment to our lives. Why don't we have them? Because we are exactly where we want to be and have exactly what we want at this point in time. Let me explain.

First of all, there is nothing wrong with being satisfied with what we have or what we are doing with our lives. I believe it is an unnecessary burden to live with "more is better," and that one should always be striving toward unnecessary improvement in life. It is okay to be satisfied. It is not okay, however, to be satisfied because we believe there is nothing we can do to alter our circumstances. This is nothing more than living by default. That is the point I'm addressing. We are and have the lives we do as the direct result of choices, which are the direct result of beliefs and values. I used to say to those groups of unhappily single people that they all could have a spouse in a reasonable short period of time if that was really what they most wanted. You should have seen the reactions. It is quite simple, just settle for anything. Take the first person who shows any interest, regardless of age, appearance, lifestyle, income level, social circumstances, suitability, or any of the usually important qualifiers. If marriage is the absolutely most important condition to be realized, it can be achieved, but that goal must absolutely overshadow any other consideration. Period.

Of course the average thinking person responds to this perspective with less than a confident embrace. It is ridiculous, and incredulous to think that we would abdicate the position of reason or the things we value, just to have a spouse. But that is the whole point. We are where we are circumstantially, because of the choices we make, based on the values and principles which are important to us. Let's say you value financial solvency. It is unlikely that if you make under $50,000 a year, that you will go out and purchase a new Mercedes-Benz SL Coupe for $100,000. I have known people with less than honest inclinations who manage to manipulate deals and financing in such a way as to drive off the lot in an expensive car with little likelihood of being able to keep up with the obligation. They got what they wanted, at the cost of manipulation, deceit and misrepresentation. They also eventually got what they created; some form of financial disaster, repossession, or other upheavals. To tell this person that this was exactly what he wanted, sounds bizarre. However, this individual exercised volitional choices, in a manner he wanted to, therefore the results must be his responsibility, or the preferred (albeit perhaps unconscious) outcome. It goes something like, "Even though there is hassle in this process, at least I get what I want, and I will not think about anything else."

The unhappy single person deliberately chooses singleness over other alternatives. Therefore he is not the hapless victim of a poor male/female ratio of decent people. The person driving a car which looks like it belongs to his less-than-with-it father instead of one reflecting good taste and style is doing so by choice. The person working a $20,000-a-year job, instead of one for $50,000 or $100,000 is also exercising deliberate choice.

Reality, of course, indicates that not everyone can waltz into a Fortune 500 Company and demand a six-figure annual income. Reality also indicates that everyone is capable and provided with ample opportunity to make choices to set the stage to create opportunity for other choices. We operate with an evil myth if we come to believe that the good and wonderful opportunities in life are just available at random to a lucky few. We must make certain choices, sometimes difficult and expensive in terms of time and effort, if we are to provide ourselves with the opportunity for other choices.

To say we are exactly where we want to be is reflective of our willingness to pay prices for those choices and opportunities. To say that there is no one to marry isn't true. To choose not to marry a jerk is a good choice, but continued singleness is the immediate consequence, therefore the chosen outcome. The point in identifying this as a choice result, is that we are not only involved in the choice, but have the choice to be involved in how we manage the consequence of that choice. That perception keeps us from having to manage the feelings of victimization. To choose to not stretch to acquire an expensive car is perhaps a disappointment, but not something over which one has no control or choice. To struggle in changing an aspect of our lives we know we should but don't is also reflective of choices, perhaps not so much involving gain, but loss.

I was talking with a middle-aged professional some time ago who was chastising himself about his lack of success in quitting smoking. As we talked, he reflected on how he knew it was bad for him, that his health was already showing the effects, how he knew he would feel better, have more energy if he quit, but just couldn't seem to get past some obstacles. As we talked, I suggested to him that there was likely a great benefit for him in not stopping this habit. His incredulous look at me prompted another question: "What would you loose if you quit?"

"Absolutely nothing" was his knee-jerk verbal response. However, being the honest and sincere person he is, he started to think out loud: "Well, it is one of the things my wife and I do together, it is a common enjoyment we have ..." and as he continued to share his thoughts, it became clear what some of his resistance was. Rather than being a failure at quitting smoking, he was being a success at maintaining a part of his relationship with his wife.

By identifying the resistance we have to change, we give ourselves the ability to make deliberate choices, to embrace purposeful perspectives and to give a new and targeted message to our subconscious. We can be respondents to whatever change we do stimulate and address the shifts that do occur.

The secondary benefit is that we no longer have to wonder what is wrong with us or why we are so deficient in trying to accomplish something. We simply remove the necessity to not change. We take away the unknown intimidators which seduce us with the idea that we cannot afford to do something which we know to be good for us. Being "good for us" is generally not adequate motivation. We must absolutely believe that two things will occur: first, that the change will be of great enough value, and second, that it won't cost us too much in whatever terms we're measuring.

Someone once said that to be successful, you must "Plan your work, and work your plan." In the context of change, this means planning the choices you must make to set the stage for making the future choices you really want to make. Let's say that financial independence is a personal goal that represents the way in which you would really like to live. That goal suggests there will need to be specific choices made in order to accomplish that outcome. For some people that may mean driving an older but serviceable car, renting an apartment instead of the purchase of an expensive home, going to night school, investing income, things which are not particularly glamorous or exciting. It is far more fun to drive a new exotic car, live in a home you are purchasing, having evening and weekends free, and enjoying spending whatever money you make. In varying degrees, either lifestyle is available to anyone. These are all the result of choices made, based on our level of comfort, and our belief about actually being able to accomplish the goal. This again is where the perceptions we use to process this experience are so critically important.

*Where we are in life is more a reflection of what we believe about ourselves than anything else.* Our willingness to risk, stretch, investigate, and become uncomfortable is a product of the perceptions we have, the ability to conceptualize ourselves in a totally, or even partially, different environment, and doing well in it. To visualize exactly where we want to be is to be immediately confronted with our beliefs about several things, among them our own personal value, what we deserve, if we fit in the picture, what other people will think or say about us in the picture, if we have the staying power to remain in the picture, or is the wish a flash in the pan, and do we dare risk the disappointment and embarrassment if it doesn't happen.

It's actually easier to dream about something never realized, than it is to try and then know it will never happen. This is perhaps one of the most pervasive arguments for not getting off of the dime. The ego would rather say, "Well, I could have if I really wanted to," than "I am not capable." That statement, "I am not capable" is more often a less stressful assessment of ourselves than a willingness to take a perceptual risk of how we will view ourselves. The unhappy fact is that too many people never find out the truth—the discovery of the talent, ability, and accomplishments which lie still undiscovered. The price tag again is often the issue — finding out will be uncomfortable for a while.

I have a friend who owns a successful men's clothing store, which he has operated for many years with a relentless determination to provide the absolute best in men's clothing. His underlying commitment is to cater to those who expect the very best. He hasn't wavered from that premise, and it has paid off. It has also cost. It has meant discomfort during times when it may have seemed to make more sense to lower his standards to accommodate a different and larger market share. I'm sure, there were times when he was tempted to drop his original values and capitulate to the cheaper and easier. But he refused to alter his commitment to quality and he became successful. Too many people give in to temporary discomfort and abandon the ideal that inspired them.

I am proud of my friend and inspired by him and others I know who keep on. They are the talented tight-rope walkers who occasionally have to move their hands around and shift their body position to adjust and maintain balance.

There is a story about plowing fields. It says to plow straight rows, you must fix your focus on a distant point and not waver your perspective. Looking at what is immediately around you will take you everywhere but in a straight line.

If we develop and embrace a perception of change as a condition of life, not as signals to alter significant choices or commitments, we will succeed in the ongoing shaping and realization of our goals and dreams. My friend's success with his clothing store has had little to do with his location. Many of his best customers come from a major city about 50 miles away. Nor is his pricing advantageous. A mutual friend quipped when he looked at the prices: "Man, he's proud of these clothes!" His success comes more from a foundational belief, a set of what I would call "Processing Perceptions" that keep him committed to a business ideal and philosophy to provide excellence in products and service, and to continue to adjust and be creative in response to changes that threaten to challenge his commitment to excellence. He demonstrates the contagious quality of exposure to excellence and the resulting inspiration spills over into other areas of his life experience which are not even related.

Like my friend, if we are going to be happy, healthy and functional, we must deliberately match our perceptions to views that allow us to stay mobile and creative, rather than scared and paralyzed.

Processing perceptions are those which remain always in our psychological tool-bag. They are deliberately chosen beliefs which we purposefully apply to situations that are unwelcome, confusing, disappointing or surprising. They automatically answer the question: "How to I want to look at this situation?" These perceptions vary from person to person depending on the specific outcomes we want to achieve. There are however at the same time, those which have universal value and function for all of us at all times.

As an example, we could say that the primary processing perception of a car salesman is to process all questions, inquiries and resistances with a view to closing the sale. If the salesman processed all responses from a standpoint of measuring how his prospective buyer's life was going, how he was feeling that day, how well the buyer liked him as a salesperson, he would likely close few, if any, sales. Those inherent values in that processing style are okay values; they are however inconsistent with the desired outcome. That does not suggest that we should be insensitive and boorish. Rather that we include the values of human decency and stay clear on what we want the outcome to be and view the events accordingly. If the prospective buyer doesn't want to buy today, he will buy sometime. How we treat him affects whether he buys from us or not. To sell, is not to force. It is to provide forward moving responses to objections and resistances, to perceive the process as necessary, and that the customer has the right to do anything he wants to do. It is to grant the privilege of non-coercive choice, and not to see ourselves as the loser if the sale doesn't close. A processing perception says, "I helped my customer answer questions, established rapport and trust, and have done well to keep the door open by making this a good experience for him." In other words, no one lost.

If we are having to work hard to sell a product, it may well be that the product itself demands a hard sell. Living effectively includes the awareness of what kinds of circumstances we put ourselves in that make the desired outcome harder to achieve than necessary. It does little good to try to learn how to sell a particular product more effectively if the product has limited value. That will dictate greater effectiveness at manipulation and coercion. The obvious often escapes us — match the quality of the product to the quality of the outcome we want. In other words, if you don't want to work so hard at selling, find or create something that sells itself.

To say that we are exactly where we want to be, is perhaps to say that we are where we are comfortable, or where we subconsciously believe we should be. The car salesman has a choice over how to label his view of the customer driving off in the same car he drove in. He can say, "I will choose to look at this customer as someone with whom I won rather than lost." A commission is great — perhaps the main reason he is there. However, his ultimate success depends on processing this experience in a way that is consistent with the ultimate outcome. If that, by the way, is to sell a car to everyone who drives on the lot, everybody involved in the process will be unhappy.

What we need to understand is that there is the opportunity for being purposeful about that position, rather than positioning by default or as a result of subconscious maneuvering accomplished by our beliefs or the desire for comfort. A willingness to acknowledge this reality eliminates any sense of victimization, or being out of control of the direction of our lives in any undertaking. It empowers a person to move toward whatever desired outcome he values. This is one of those generalized processing perceptions which refuse to allow us to feel controlled by the variable in any of our experiences. It is certainly okay to be disappointed about events which do not go the way we would like them to. On the other hand, some of the best things I've ever experienced have been on the heels of disappointment, and the circumstantial redirection toward something I couldn't even see as an opportunity before things went sideways in my plans.

If we want a life which is more colorful, enriching and rewarding, we are exactly where we want to be as things around us change, shift and surprise us. It is not the process we want and welcome, it is the arena of opportunity to move toward the things we want. To want, to desire, to hope and to dream is to deliberately move into the world of confusion, uncertainty, circumstantial shifts, exhilaration, disappointment and the adrenaline rush that enhances both fear and joy. The failure to accept this perception and integrate it into how we process things which happen, is to constantly remain confused about why things happen as they do. They are a part of the program. They also facilitate the very change we want. The biblical letter to James starts with: "When trouble and adversity comes your way, embrace and welcome it as a friend, because it serves to stimulate growth and change" (my paraphrase).

This perspective finally gives us all an answer to the knee-jerk question we all ask when things go wrong—"Why?" Those things happen because we have entered into contract with life to not live inside of a safe little secure box. Everything we experience which "goes wrong" is a testimony to a willingness to be alive, try things, take and manage risks, and learn to live a life consistent with our dreams and goals. This applies to kid problems, marriage problems, business problems, weight problems, people problems, homeowner problems, tax problems, anything which is a part of our life experience. We have made choice to enter into these arenas, and therefore experience the full spectrum of participating in those choices. That does not leave us victims, but rather with the choice to learn and exercise problem-solving skills to resolve or survive the experience. As long as we don't waste time protesting the experience, we'll have energy to resolve or manage those situations.

"Why?" becomes an unnecessary question to spend good time with. "How?" allows us to continue to move, with the hope of a reasonable outcome. You are presently exactly where you want to be, given current expectations, beliefs and perception. It is not necessary to wonder why you're there, rather, be deliberate in making informed and conscious choices about the outcomes you want and start to use deliberate perceptions to keep you on track. "I will make it," "We will survive." "It will happen." "I will not quit." "There has to be a way." These are a few of those consistent perceptual responses we need to exercise. If we do that, there is no question whatsoever about the outcome.

As long as we don't equate the process of getting there with the outcome, we'll be fine. In other words, pain in the process doesn't mean a painful outcome, and conversely, a happy outcome doesn't mean a happy process of getting there.

## *Summary*

The quality of your life at this point in time is the successful outcome of choices that have been made before. You are already living successfully, regardless of what circumstances may appear to be, in that you are living out the outcomes of those previous choices. The opportunity now is to recognize that new choices will also lead to new outcomes. Made one new choice that is pointed in the direction you would want your life to result within a specific time line, i.e., one month, one year.

# 6

## *Power Brokering; The Use And Balance Of Personal Power*

The satisfaction of beginning to manage our lives in more productive ways comes from understanding the factors at work. Getting a clear and deliberate focus on what we want to accomplish is certainly the starting point. Beyond that, one of the most significant tools in terms of changing our own emotional and circumstantial results, is the matter of understanding our personal power, how to exercise it, and not unintentionally give it away. Personal power begins with a belief: If we believe we have the ability to influence our circumstances, we do. If, on the other hand, we believe ourselves incapable of exercising any influence or control, we simply withdraw from the process, therefore we don't.

It is really a very simple issue, either we have and exercise personal power, or we don't. The sense of power to effect change creates hope and optimism. A sense of powerlessness on the other hand, creates a whole range of negative emotions and outlooks. It is also the perceived inability to do anything about our circumstances.

The sense of power, or powerlessness, and the perceptions that accompany them, are at the same time perceptions, beliefs and habits. For example, if we believe a situation is unchangeable, it becomes exactly that. Because we invest no energy to shift the direction of what is occurring, it remains static. A lifestyle "habit" of resignation emerges in response to any number of situations. The underlying belief states: "I have no ability to change this situation." So we develop a powerless response pattern. "I can't do anything about it," becomes a familiar and comfortable view. The first thought is not, "What can I do about this?" but, "Why are these things always happening to me?" This is the foundation of an attitude that looks to other people to solve our problems, fix things and take responsibility for our discomfort.

On the other hand, a belief that dictates that something can always be done, some answer exists, nothing has the power to stop us, will create action as natural as taking a breath. If there is an absolute refusal to accept the potential impairment of a circumstance, regardless of its intensity, proactive movement will be an eventual response.

Realistically, some things hurt. Others set us back on our heels for a while. Some things wound and need time to heal. So, it is not whether or not you get moving again immediately after something goes south on you, it's just a matter of time before that perspective creates that restlessness to do something about what's happened.

Of the many wonderful clients I work with, some of the most delightful are the kids. Frequently, they are brought to me by good parents who are understandably frustrated by the normal quirks and kinks of adolescence. The often unstated, "Help," or "Can you fix him" is seen in the desperate look on their faces.

This was the case with the adopted daughter of a single woman. The girl was strong-willed, combative, believed that she was always treated unfairly and was highly manipulative. Her mother was also strong-willed, but out of a sense of guilt and personal uncertainty was overly accommodating with her daughter and generally unsure about whether her parenting decisions were right.

It was clear to me when I first interviewed mother and daughter that whenever there was a discussion between the two over an issue of privilege, an opportunity, or a matter of obligation for the child, war started. Because the mother had sabotaged her own authority by being too permissive and accommodating, the question of "Who's in charge?" became a real one. Uncomfortable with anyone being mad at her, the parent's habitual response to conflict was to give in, or, to use my words, "give away power."

This capable mother was unwittingly brokering away her power. On a daily basis she gave away, exchanged or wasted her personal power with her daughter. She did that by assuming that she must be doing something wrong if her daughter was so upset. She lived with several underlying perceptions about conflict. After all, "if you do everything right, everyone will always be happy with you! If they're not happy, you'd better do something about it." And the recipient of her power enjoyed regular victories, but had absolutely no ability to manage the responsibility of the power. In this case, the parent was not only losing, but was being in a unique way, abusive. It is an abusive gesture, I believe, to put power in the hands of someone who does not have the ability to manage it. She was simply teaching her daughter to challenge power and authority, and that she could expect it to capitulate.

The key issue was that the mother had no sense of the power of being either decisive or indecisive. She didn't realize that she encouraged, even insisted on this power struggle, because of her own unwillingness to let her daughter be upset, and not take the responsibility for those feelings the young girl demonstrated. The expression of the daughter's feelings, whether rage, hurt, frustration or despair, were all solicitations for the mother to do something. It wasn't just to capitulate; it was to give the power to her to then control the family. Children cannot rule a family unless the power is given to them. This generous mother did it abundantly.

Having and retaining power is not rigidity. Giving it away is not kindness. Nor is it a demonstration of love, care, interest or support. It takes a focused sense of self to be clear about the balance of power in any type of relationship. If a person's self esteem is wrapped up in someone else's approval, the potential for disapproval carries with it tremendous power. That power will confuse the picture of the healthy outcomes we want, as well as the means of getting there. What people often fail to recognize is that to be human is to be self-serving at some level. Thus, the use and balance of power is important.

It is absolutely necessary if we are to function with healthy perspectives that we operate from a position of balanced power. One of the best ways to understand how to do this is to think in terms of a "line of responsibility." We are on one side of that line; everybody and everything else is on the other side. In facing this line we encounter one of the most critical points in the balance of power and focus.

This was put in perspective a number of years ago by the psychologist William Glasser, who wrote a book about his view of mental health and its treatment called *Reality Therapy*. He stated that there are two basic themes in mental health which can be separated by a line that places personal responsibility on one side and the responsibility of others on the other side. If you are to provide a sense of balance in your life, whether emotional, perceptual or with regard to power, you must first be willing to assume complete, absolute and undeniable responsibility for ALL of your choices, behaviors, feelings, perspectives, attitudes and all that is within your mind and heart. No one, nor anything else is to blame for those experiences and your reactions to them.

The other side of the line represents the equal responsibility of others to do the same. Important to this division is that we can't step in and take, or allow to be handed to us, any of the responsibility for the feelings, choices, actions or perspectives of others.

This also implies that if someone on the other side of that line does not pick up his responsibility, it must stay that way. If we pick it up, or try to facilitate it, we start the vicious circle of confused responsibility all over again. We have the wrong people doing the wrong things for the wrong reasons with the wrong results.

What does all of this have to do with power? It has to do with learning how to keep the power of our choices and perspectives in our own hands, not to give it away by stepping over the line of responsibility. It means not assuming responsibility for the way somebody else sees a situation, which dictates our reactions to his perceptions. It also means that someone else's expectations, desires and goals are his — maybe they're good, but they still belong to him. We have to decide to accept, reject and make them ours or not. Without a clear resolution to that issue, we're left to struggle with guilt, frustration, disappointment in ourselves, or some other unnecessary and time-wasting turmoil.

A fascinating client I worked with was a successful stock broker for one of the well known national firms. While in his early forties he had made a successful transition from another field. At the time I saw him he had been in his new position for about four years. His problems were depression and anxiety over being able to continue to keep up his level of performance. As a newcomer to the business, he already was among the top performers.

As we began to investigate the issues which were undermining his focus and putting his success at risk, a couple of interesting points surfaced. He had always been a self starter. He been successful at whatever he had done. He had always functioned independently without the need for supervision. In his new position, however, he faced clearly stated expectations — including implied policies about when he should be on the phone, how many cold calls he should make, and during what hours it should take place.

What happened was he inadvertently embraced someone else's perceptions of himself and his abilities. He stepped over that personal line of responsibility and tried to "own" someone else's view of how to be successful. Simply put, it was, "You need someone to tell you what to do, when and how to do it." This shift in the power of his actions undermined two important elements of effectiveness. One was his confidence in himself to be productive, which had never before been an issue; the other was the freedom to be decisive and act on his own sense of what needed to be done.

We worked to give him some awareness of what was happening, and some practical tools to turn this power inversion around. As we talked, we discovered a symbol for his frustration and sense of pressure. It was a large clock hanging on the wall over his desk. The clock was reinforcing the message to him: "Without me or someone else telling you what to do and when to do it, you'll fail. Besides, it is my job to get you going, and when I say 8:00 a.m., you had better jump and get with it!"

The clock had inadvertently been given the power to make him think that he couldn't function without it. Its voice was so penetrating, that he couldn't remember that he had never in his life needed a timepiece to prompt him to action. We decided to have a conversation with the clock every morning. Well, it wasn't really a conversation, more of a gesture!

He started every day with that gesture toward the clock. I can still remember the smile on his face, and our tear-prompting laughter as he recounted his new morning ritual. In this simple identification of misapplied power, and a way to perceive his situation differently, he took back his power, and experienced again a great sense of freedom to act on what he used to believe — that he was in fact capable to manage himself well.

His declaration was, "I will believe nothing less than that I am completely capable of doing what I want to do without any pressure from you. Get lost!" In that simple declaration, he recaptured an accurate sense of himself and came alive. His perceptions had reattached themselves to an appropriate belief.

I saw him about a year later to discuss another issue. He was still on track, producing well and hardly noticing the clock. He took back power, and it rewarded him well.

It seems that the more sensitive and caring a person is, the more there is a tendency to fall victim to stepping over the line we're discussing. Because you may care about how another feels, and may be empathetic about his feelings, it is easy to say to yourself, "Well, if he feels that way, I should do something about it." We must absolutely not violate this line. It is one thing to be in a situation where there are reasonable expectations of us. It is another matter to give away the power of choice by vacating our own healthy perceptions. The unfortunate message you often communicate is: "If you're unhappy about something, let me know and I'll do something to make you feel better."

What's wrong with that? Nothing if the unhappy person is an infant! Everything, if he is of an age to make decisions and able to understand what he can do about the situation. "I'm sorry you feel that way," is an appropriate and clear response to stay within the responsibility boundaries. Here, in fact, is one of the dilemmas of parenting: "When does this shift in power and responsibility take place?" As parents our actions and choices certainly affect our children—decisions about the time they go to bed, types and extent of their privileges, how we handle moods and disappointments. Also, we are responsible for providing a safe and secure environment for them. We must teach our children to gradually accept responsibility as to how they interpret the environment, respond to it, feel about it and about us, as their parents.

If we teach them to deal with their environment by challenging it, and to expect us to adapt it to meet their challenges, we've taught them that their happiness and feelings are our responsibility. If on the other hand, we respond with understanding about how they feel, listen to their concerns, but stay focused on who is responsible for our happiness and for theirs, we create a much healthier environment with clear boundaries for emotional and perceptual well-being.

An old Chinese proverb states this point well: "If you want to feed a man for a day, catch him a fish. If you want to feed him for a lifetime, teach him how to fish." My point is about managing power and perceptions. Will we manage our own, and teach others the same, or try to manage others by our reactions, accommodations and overly pleasing gestures (which create disrespect anyway)? "Teaching people to fish" is best done by learning ourselves the issues involved in maintaining healthy perspectives and demonstrating the same to those with whom we live and interact.

Power brokering is not so bad as long as we know who gets power for what. This is one of the areas where we unnecessarily complicate or confuse things for ourselves. To put it simply, we must take the responsibility for our own happiness, peace of mind, dreams and financial condition. It also means the responsibility to not set in our own way the obstacles of circumstances and perceptions which we then later have to spend so much time trying to manage.

Power was the subject of the guest on a radio talk show I happened to tune in the other day while I was driving down the freeway. He said: "Part of the benefit of becoming powerful is believing you're powerful." When you embrace that belief it becomes a wonderful tool to use as a foundation for any kind of change we want to create. It also takes a leap of faith to embrace a posture which believes that we do in fact have power to create meaningful change. It is not until that leap of faith, sometimes maybe more like a crawl, that we begin to collect evidence that it can in fact happen.

Remember, that it is also a leap of faith to say, "It can't happen." That is a chosen perspective, equally arbitrary, but equally full of power to create evidence that it is true.

Power, then, means finding a perspective that is consistent with the results you want, keep it clearly in focus through whatever helps you to do so, and keep the boundaries of responsibility for its outcome firmly and consistently intact.

A part of moving forward in anything, is the ability to change your mind. The kind of power we're discussing is important to the decision of changing the direction of a previous decision. In other words, we retain a healthy perspective on personal power by making a deliberate choice to stop or redirect. This is not a decision by default, because something isn't working. It is rather an informed decision in which you say, "I choose to not do this any longer because it is not in my best interest, nor is it consistent with my long term goals." We cannot afford the definition of success which always deals with difficult situations with the "never-say-die" attitude. It is not effective living or a demonstration of personal power to ignore the reality of something that is not working. We cannot afford a definition of failure that includes anything that needs to shift, change or simply stop. Successful living must include the wide-eyed prudence of monitoring the trends of what we are working toward, and a willingness to define things not working as just that — they're not working. Not a definition of oneself, one's abilities, or one's hope for a future. We create a perceptual quagmire for ourselves if we create definitions of the outcomes we undertake as the means to define ourselves or our future. Power, the ability to do something about whatever is happening, must be built on a foundation which includes the deliberate perception that says; the only failure, is to not respond and exercise new choices.

How we then label that redirecting action is critically important.

If we tell ourselves (remember, your subconscious believes everything you tell it) that we're changing directions because we blew it, failed miserably, made a stupid decision or just did another bone-headed thing, we are doing nothing more than reinforcing perceptions of ourselves that will keep us living in the same old circles of frustration. On the other hand, to tell yourself, that your are simply exercising a new choice, based on new information, new circumstances, new priorities, you will walk away with your personal power, and your direction intact.

This focus of power has great significance in all levels of relationships. The ability to maintain intimacy for example, is highly dependent on the management of power in a significant relationship. There must be a balance of power for intimacy to exist. In a partnership, equality and safety are measured in the distribution of power. If we are clear on the use of balanced power in our own lives, it is not necessary to dominate or subjugate in an adult relationship. In the absence of clearly understood boundaries and roles, power imbalances are inevitable with unproductive results. The demise of the Soviet Union demonstrates the point well. The "child" grew up and needed to redefine the hierarchal relationship. What we now witness is the chaos and upheaval which is the direct result of decades of choiceless existence — nothing is yet working. With little successful experience in the former Soviet Union in personal or communal choices, chaos continues. Having no anchor in experience, the idealism of freedom is at risk of returning to the unpleasant but familiar structure indicating absence of choice. Discomfort is a powerful voice against change.

The ability to come together and redefine any relationship, means an understanding of the boundaries of power. The exercise of power does not mean that one person or group wins, and the other loses. Demonstrating power is not getting your way. It is a willingness to watch out for your own interests, and be willing to integrate the need of someone else's as well. It has been described in other contexts as Win/Win. The inability to accomplish that end means continual struggle or failure.

In some of the consulting work I do with businesses, frequent issues and problems come up around this theme. One client I worked with owned a successful chain of stores. He and his brother were the principals. They had been in business together for a number of years and had reached an enviable level of accomplishment.

This client had actually come to see me for something which initially seemed unrelated to his business. However as we began that inevitable journey of discovery, we ran into the issue of power. One day he was expressing some frustration about his role in their firm. He was the go-for. He did a lot of the unglamorous grunt work. Much of his energy was spent in time consuming follow up to make sure things were done. On top of that, he had the smallest office of the two brother/partners. That really stuck in his craw.

It wasn't that his brother/partner had even insisted on any of this structure. At first glance it looked as though it had just happened, and evolved on its own. Further investigation however, told a different story. My client hated conflict and confrontation. He would do almost anything not to make waves. He would accommodate, go the extra mile, take on the extra work, give more benefits to someone else, all to avoid stress. This man was totally stressed out over all of this. He was usually agitated, quick tempered and reactive. He had a difficult time listening, was absorbed with his perspective of being victimized and vented volumes of toxic emotional waste.

What was also true, was that this pattern of giving away the power of being able to maintain a balanced role in his business, permeated every other part of his life. The operational perception he worked with was distorted. His underlying belief was that his value and worth was less than those significant people in his life, therefore they should get the best deal. His own sense of self worth also dictated to him that unless he gave these people who were important to him what they wanted, he would probably lose them. This of course was not a consciously stated belief; it would be obviously ridiculous. That belief did, however, dictate his perception about how corporate decisions should be made, who should get the most perks, who in his personal life should have the most flexibility, and what perks he deserved to enjoy in life.

He continually put the power of his well being, his opportunities, his roles, and ultimately his life into the hands of those who really didn't want it anyway. These people were bewildered at his anger, agitation and occasional blow ups. He was venting the regularly accumulating frustration of "taking it in the shorts." This did not mean he had to turn 180 degrees and become demanding and take the power away from everyone else. It just meant learning how not to give away what he needed to stay balanced, and stop creating the situations for himself which perpetuated the vicious circle of accommodation, disappointment, anger, venting, guilt, etc.

This client gave me another large installment of value in my role of helping people. As the light bulbs of awareness came on, he began to shift his roles. It took risking to deal with others differently, and believing that the outcome might be different — for everyone's well being. Perhaps the greatest risk was in believing that he was worth it. All of this boiled down to understanding the issue of the function of personal power. He stopped giving it away as an indiscriminate reflex. He retained it as an essential ingredient to be able to manage his life and business.

Of the many demonstrations of power, choice is perhaps the most significant. The power of choice, it must be realized, is not demonstrated by a guaranteed outcome, other than the ability to choose. Choice represents the freedom to accept, protest, cooperate, fight, or to embrace as our own the reality in front of us — welcome or not. "I have no choice" is the confession of a victim. "I can't do anything about this," is just a statement reflecting an unwillingness to look at the available choices. The subconscious believes every confession it hears. We are therefore continually programming and training ourselves to work with whatever perception the subconscious is forced to listen to. To believe that alternatives are not available, just because we cannot control the end result, is to confess to hopelessness: Other people have the power to withhold authority, influence and accomplishments from us. But, outcome does NOT decide power or powerlessness; decisions however most certainly do. You can choose how you will respond. That is the exercise of power.

One of the epic stories in human history is about the life of Christ. His claims and demonstration of the "God become man," "The

Son of God," are hardly supported if we were to measure power by the consequences He experienced. He demonstrated little in the conventional sense. He was rejected by the religious leaders in the community in which He was to have been a voice. He seemed to have little influence on the political infrastructure that regarded Him as a threatening nuisance. He was certainly not popular among the social elite. His friends were not politically correct. He was finally arrested, judged, and eliminated from the social conscience. Done deal.

Yet the historical account of Him being judged by Pilate bears some insightful gems of His personal power. Here's the picture: He is in court, being judged by a politically pressured official, and He knows what is going to happen. In a circumstance over which He had no choice His perspective was: *"You can't take my life. I will give it to you."*

The psychotherapists in the crowd would certainly have diagnosed Him as being in denial about the seriousness of His situation. The psychiatrists would have suspected some delusional disorder, robbing Him of reality. The lawyers would have wondered at His strategy of confusion and misplaced power and volunteered their services to save Him from Himself. The religious leaders would have delighted in the pending failure of this self-appointed Messiah. The judge would certainly have pondered his own sense of helplessness in this apparent moment of potent high drama. But Jesus understood that He was in charge of His life. He took the inevitable and redefined it to His terms. The ironic victims were those who did not know how to respond to the confusion created by the power Jesus demonstrated. He retained power in what was perhaps the most powerless situation in which any person could find himself. To put it simply, His power was in acknowledging the reality of what was happening, and in making a choice that went beyond resignation.

This principle does not involve capitulation. Nor does it accept the role of victim. It rather recognizes the uncomfortable reality, then makes a choice of posture in those events that are out of our control.

Choice is not the only broker of power. Its ally is something I'll call "Filters." Filters determine what gets in, and what stays out. They have a variety of applications, from furnaces, to engines, to our minds and perceptions. The filters we're going to look at keep out unwanted material.

However, these filters also allow in those "materials" which are beneficial. In the case of mental filters, they are represented by thoughts, beliefs, and perceptions consistent with goals or desired outcomes. One client I worked with already held a corporate position. While living a comfortable life as a whole, he wanted to change the direction of his professional activity. He did his homework well. He hired a consulting firm to help him do a market analysis, including a survey of the industry he wanted to work with in the future. The information he received was generally encouraging, but nothing to make him run out and leave his present position immediately. Slowly he developed a game plan to begin a consulting practice.

Several things then happened. The manager of the company he worked for started making waves about any of the employees doing outside consulting work, a commonplace practice in this industry. Consequently, their schedules were monitored, cellular calls were scrutinized, and they were generally on notice to spend all of their professional energy "at home." This client of mine suddenly had some choices to make. The issues now at hand could be sending him any number of different messages: "Stop what you're doing, before you put your job at risk," or "Just keep a low profile, and they'll not notice," or "What right does he have to control my time as long as I'm doing what's required. I'm just going to keep doing what I want."

This is the starting point of formulating perceptions: "How am I going to look at what is happening?" Which of those messages, or others, are listened to will dictate the perceptual view, and have an effect on what will eventually happen. Historically, he would have made choices from what I would call "Fear-based perception." He would have looked at this office situation and chosen to look at those facts as reasons why he couldn't do what he wanted, at least without leaving the company. However, he now made some different choices.

Rather than give up developing his consulting practice or simply avoid the situation and hope for the best, he made a concrete choice to look at the situation in a way that would work for him — what I call a

"Power-based perception." He held tenaciously to the perspective he wanted — there was some way to accomplish this without leaving his job. He then clarified the time expectations of him by this company, and then took a risk. He stated to this company that he would be doing limited outside work, but that it would not be conducted during normal business hours. He did not take away their choice about his activity, but was clear, determined and willing to take some measure of risk. They did not press the issue.

He hired an answering service to manage the incoming calls from the business he was generating. He checked those messages during normal breaks allowed in his present schedule. He acquired an additional cellular phone and number so that when he was on the road, which was regular duty with much "dead time," he could follow up with calls to his new clients. The new work he was doing was easily managed by preparing documents and information a couple of evenings a week, and a few leisurely hours over the weekend. By the way, his regular position was basically contained in a forty-hour week. His extra consulting activities caused little impact on the other things which were also important to maintain — quality family time.

The point he illustrates is that in maintaining a position of power, through perceptions, beliefs and actions he did not do this at anyone else's expense. All the people in his life got what they needed. Accomplishing this balance and success started with a power-based perception: "I will not let these new events tell me what is going to happen; I will manage them and find a way to make it work." He understood the potential price tag, but reconciled himself to it, not as a victim of something he couldn't control, but simply as a potential consequence for his exercising a choice of great value. We have to keep the value in focus or we get lost.

I like the idea of reframing. Basically it suggests that we take a picture, remove the existing frame (perception), and replace it with a more workable or useful one. If you've ever tried to redecorate your home or office, you know how much difference the right frame can make. The interesting thing to me is that the basic picture itself has not changed, nor even been retouched or slightly altered. It has just been presented differently. It has been placed in a different frame of reference, in a different context, and now it works. What was once unuseful, perhaps even undesirable, has now become something that is either tolerable or valued. You can now move forward, relieved of the burden of something imposing itself on you. You have redefined it, made it serve your purposes, and not lost power at all over its impact on you.

I experienced two firsts this year. One was an I.R.S. audit. The other was a nasty neighbor problem. Both went on for what seemed to be an interminable length of time. If time flies when you're having fun, it most certainly drags when you're not. These events were not fun.

Let's start with Uncle Sam. The timing of notification was just great. One week before Christmas. First meeting, Christmas Eve day. They couldn't wait. When the field agent called me at my office, his attempts at levity were certainly well intended I'm sure, but I wasn't amused. He gave me one of these "Good news, Bad News" shots.

"Are you the Raymond J. Watson of such and such address? Is your Social Security number such and such?" His "Good News" was that he had the right guy. My bad news was that I was going to be audited. Merry Christmas! It had not been the best of years already. This was actually the perfect way to end such a wearisome year.

About the only reframing filter I could come up with during my bad news recovery was something like, "Well, if it's going to happen, it might as well be this year and just get it over with." For a variety of reasons, including significant turnover in our local I.R.S. office, the audit took several months, and a number of meetings to resolve. The first one by the way was a seven and one half hour marathon. By the time I got through, I couldn't remember my name, much less what I did with my money three years ago. The agent was just getting warmed up. He was in his glory!

Eventually, with much help from my accountant, and fortunately good documentation, the audit was concluded "No Change." There is a God! In retrospect, the process did me a favor. I learned a lot about how to keep the kind of records which would have made the process a relative breeze. I learned a great deal about the problem areas in returns which represent, as in my case, more than one *Schedule C* business. I also learned "Trust the Professionals." I keep forgetting the last one.

Oh yes, my neighbor. I live in an equestrian-oriented community. There had been some discussion about the use of common areas in our development. After what at first seemed to be a reasonable resolution, something went wrong. All of a sudden I was inundated with letters from city and county officials about all kinds of alleged violations and problems. My initial reactions was "What on earth is this all about?" I later discovered, somewhat by accident, that the source of all of this was a neighbor who became the "Neighbor from Hell." I was less than enthused about being thrust into a neighborhood battle. It wasn't pleasant thinking about having to deal with bureaucratic officials. You know, "You can't beat City Hall" anticipation.

In any event, the process of getting the issues resolved has been interesting. Contrary to popular opinion, the officials involved have proven very helpful allies. What started out as an intimidating and threatening process has been resolved with a great sense of support and help from an unexpected source, City Hall. The "Neighbor from Hell" stirred up a mess, but eventually to her own embarrassment, did our community a favor by demonstrating to everyone involved how toxic she really was. She lost the power of gossip, manipulation and control of people's information.

The core issue is again one of focus. It boils down to two basic options: One, roll over, and let whatever happens happen, and two, there must be some way to get this problem resolved. Whichever frame we choose to put around this picture absolutely dictates the outcome. That doesn't mean that our "frame" makes it any more fun, but we can learn the benefit of not giving away whatever power we may have to at least do something. Living successfully means the choice to not be a victim.

In this discussion of power and its use, the purpose of choices and filters as agents or vehicles of personal power becomes one of important awareness. They are two non-negotiable components of the ongoing effort to function in a healthy and successful fashion. Neither can be forfeited, nor unused if we are to achieve our personal or professional goals.

## *Summary*

Take a look at how you already use personal power effectively. In other words, what are you already doing that works well to create effective parts of your life. Secondly, look at areas that may not have been working as well — see where the power of directing those areas is being diluted or given away.

# Part

# II

# 7

## *The Deciding Force*

Decisions are often difficult to make, particularly those which involve movement into unfamiliar territory. I suppose it is like bungie jumping. One is the decision to do it, the other is to actually jump. It requires thinking about merging conflicting ideas. In this case, self preservation and a thrill. We must entertain ideas about possibilities, risks and desires. It forces a commitment about how serious we really are about what we're considering. Taking a decisive stand is occasionally difficult, particularly if it involves a commitment to a position of unknown certainty or outcome. Indecision on the other hand, is the only other alternative. Indecisiveness, however, does represent some benefit. It precludes the stress of having to take a position, make a commitment, and spend the emotional energy a decision requires. In reality however, indecisiveness is a decision. This decision to non-action, or "management by default" is very expensive.

Included in the expense are the costs of never reaching a goal, never tapping into your own giftedness, not knowing if your judgment of potential in something has merit, and not joining the ranks of those who enjoy the things or experiences in life you want to have for yourself. The biggest expense of indecisiveness is the failure to bridge the gap between a dream and reality, potential and fulfillment.

Ironically, some of the most successful people I have met are those who are absolutely expert at this means of managing their lives. Of course, the outcome is less than spectacular because they get nowhere that resembles any measurable accomplishment. But they have mastered the ability to create an existence by default. The perplexing question is: "Why on earth would anybody develop such negative expertise?"

Simply put, it allows that person to manage his life consistent with what he believes. People who decide "I'm old," or "I'm past my professional prime," or "Who am I kidding that I could achieve that level of accomplishment?" will consistently make decisions based on those beliefs. Their perceptions about every opportunity that presents itself is not one of welcome, but rather a potential occasion of embarrassment, proof of ineptness, or an event which inspires discouragement and depression. Here is the perplexing value of indecision. It allows for the maintenance of a position of familiar incompleteness.

Frequently, I counsel couples whose marriages are somewhere between unhappy and intolerable. Most people approach this process with a reasonably good faith intention. They come to see what they can do to improve things. Often, however, I've witnessed another dynamic.

One husband and wife had been married for fifteen years. He was a very successful stock broker, she was a full-time house wife and mother. Their lifestyle included all of the expected trappings. Beautiful home in a prestigious neighborhood, cottage on the water, the right private schools, European cars, etc. The picture was great, but the canvas it was painted on was rotting.

The presenting problem was the husband's withdrawal from his wife, and her frustration about being able to do anything productive to put the relationship back on track. As I worked with them, I saw a circular process that kept them spinning nowhere. Her frustration about his distancing was expressed in anger, to which he responded by pulling back further, which hurt her, and she expressed in anger, etc., etc.

It was clear that he simply wanted out of the marriage. However, given his financial status, the community property laws, the likelihood of paying significant spouse and and child support, he was not about to push for a divorce. What he knew about her was that she would do anything, pay any price, to get what she wanted. On the one hand, that intimidated him in knowing what she would do if she was determined enough. On the other hand, he could use that to his advantage.

The woman was at an emotional breaking point. The couple had been in this circular pattern for years, she couldn't tolerate it any more. The children were suffering, and she didn't want to live this way any longer. The husband's unspoken strategy was: "I'll keep doing my part to be indifferent toward her, show no interest in the relationship, and take no decisive action one way or the other. It will eventually drive her nuts, and she'll do anything to get out of it — even settle for far less of my assets than I would have to give her if I started a divorce action on my own." In fact his decision was to force her to make the decisions about where this marriage had to go. His strategy was working. She was about ready to take the kids, go live with her parents, and take only the clothes on their backs.

It was interesting to watch their interaction the last time I saw them. Her level of frustration with him was so intense, that she was practically screaming at him in my office. He sat there calmly and detached. What got his attention were the words, "I've had it, I'm leaving you, take it all, I just want out." He had the presence of mind not to smile, but I saw his eyes light up and he silently said, "Finally!"

He demonstrated in clear terms the value of behavioral indecision. Had anyone confronted him about what he was doing, he would have certainly denied it, and after all, there was no quantifiable evidence that this was his strategy. By the way, he didn't have smiling eyes long. She found one of those reputed shark-like divorce attorneys. What the husband eventually discovered was the price tag on both sides of indecision. It got her to make the decision, but it cost him dearly.

The issue of decisions transfers beyond action or inaction, to the issue of perceptions as well. During the week of the 1992 Summer Olympics in Barcelona, Spain, a commentator reported an interesting side story about one of the American swimmers who, competed in several events. This young woman had historically been rated at or near the top in most of her swimming competitions. One event, however, generally gave her some trouble. In past interviews she had always made a point of saying, "I am not good at this one." Whether that comment was made out of embarrassment or just honesty, she came to realize the expense of that perception of herself. In this interview she said: "I made a decision not to say that to myself anymore. I want to change my focus and work at excelling in the event." She understood the value of a decision of perspective and made it. What is of interest is that her belief that she was inferior in the event affected her performance.

A realists would say, "That was just an honest assessment of her ability." I say that it was an honest assessment of her perceived ability. Put yourself in her swim suit. Would you train hard for an event in which you believed the outcome would be mediocre anyway? Her competitive edge was improved by a decision to filter out one thought and inject a new one. If we tell our subconscious the same thing often enough, good or bad, true or false, the message will become what I call an *Operative Truth*. That is, it becomes a foundation of belief resulting in thinking and acting out what we feel and perceive.

We cannot afford listless, meandering perceptions. They will lead us to old perception-determined outcomes, not at all representative of more focused choices.

The point to this example is: in order for a decision to work toward effective living, it must be based on clear perceptions and deliberate choice. If choice is power, then we must make sure that it is not based on someone else's opinion or preference, or reached by default.

There is another important side to our perceptions about decisions. Decisions are a source of power because they stop the emotional drain of uncertainty. Imagine for a moment that you are working at a job that involves daily conflict with the manager of your department. It's always something. He is unfair and seems to take advantage of you. You go home every day emotionally exhausted and complain about what an S. O. B. he is. You're tired, difficult to live with and depressed.

You continue to hang on to your job despite advice that you

should find a better one. Your reply to yourself is: "Good jobs are tough to find. Besides, if I start looking, somebody will find out and I might lose my job before I find a replacement."

Isn't it fascinating how easy it is to get pulled into defending something we really don't want to defend? What we often don't recognize is how expensive it is not to change. In a situation like the one I've described several things are put at risk. You loose sleep, create more stress in your relationships and your body starts to talk back. Pretty soon your ulcer says: "Hey, get to your doctor." Your spouse says, "Hey, get to your shrink, or else!" Your deteriorating energy warns: "Hey, not only do you not have energy for work, you have none for play either."

The price tag for indecision, or decision by default, is increasingly high. In order for action to take place the body has to rebel, a spouse gets impatient or something happens to create change. Most of us are reluctant partners in the decision. Any significant decision, from new perceptions and beliefs, to an important goal create at least a subconscious measurement of the risks involved. Hordes of unanswered, or unanswerable questions begin their process of annoying us into indecision. An important perception is to learn to be thankful for this unwelcomed pressure.

Most of the big decisions in life are predicated by an event that can range from unpleasant to downright awful.

The point about decisions is that we are exercising the power to make choices. The consequences of indecision are left up to a fatalistic meandering. The consequences of choice are in our hands to manage.

Some time ago I was counselling with a successful businessman. While over the years he had built a very enviable financial and business empire, his personal life was a mess. On the verge of divorce and the usual financial nightmare of sorting out who gets how much of what, he was paralyzed by indecisiveness. She was willing, he was scared.

The more he pondered the risks and issues the deeper he sank into overwhelming despair. He believed he couldn't make a decision either way, the costs were potentially too great. At one point he was willing to let the decision be made by default. Whatever she decided would be okay with him. That only made things worse. He finally began to see and feel the price tag of an unwillingness to exercise *his* choices in the situation. As he made the decision to take what was really a substantial risk to reinvest in his marriage, two things happened. First, he stopped spinning in circles and feeling like a victim. Second, he became focused on what his choices were, and how to begin to carry them out.

To condense this very involved story, within a matter of a few months life for this couple had changed drastically. He finally came to grips with a long-standing issue. His reluctance to make choices was really a central theme in most of the problems they had as a couple, and he had in his business. What is also interesting, is that he was still very successful at his business. However, achieving and maintaining that success had been hard won. He regularly set the stage for things to be far more difficult than they needed to be, because his perceptions of choices and decisions was that he would loose control of the outcomes. Learning to make a deliberate shift in looking at choices, as means of being able to more effectively manage the outcome of *his* choices rather than someone else's, became an effective tool of change.

We could also call this process one of emotional efficiency. No more "wheel spinning" around issues and getting nowhere. Time to get on with directing the energy resources we have to creating and managing the direction we want to go. No more need to internally debate the issues. Decisions are personal power. Power to move, solve, grow and change. Decisions plug the holes which sap energy, drive, ambition, creativity, hope, resolve and determination.

In my years of private flying, many experiences in the cockpit have become interesting anecdotes relating to decision making. One flight returning to Seattle from a weekend on the Oregon Coast illustrates the point well. Having departed the coast and headed inland, I flew on instruments through a large weather system of dense clouds with the tops over 20,000 feet. Normally when flying on instruments in meteorological conditions the furthermost tip of your wing is visible. On this flight I couldn't even see the outside edge of the engine nacelle no more than four feet to my left in my twin engine airplane.

What became interesting about this flight, was the immediate and abrupt departure from this cloud mass. It was like flying out of a vertical wall. Instantaneous clear blue and unobstructed sky, ground to infinity. In pilot parlance, "Severe clear." It was simultaneously startling, inspiring, shocking and invigorating. Instrument flying is like that sometimes. The visually-inhibited movement along a predetermined course, a plan to follow, but no normal sensory clues as to where you are or what is happening, demands several things of you. First, you must have the training, equipment and experience. Second, you must unequivocally choose to trust your instrumentation. The seat of your pants will lie to you without batting an eye. You must further depend on clues and input that are not a part of our normal means of determining safety, direction and outcome.

That same instrument flying makes some promises as well. There will be the unexpected — weather changes, wind direction and velocity shifts, and unforecast conditions. Further, it promises that if you follow the rules and procedures, and exercise good judgment, you will get safely to where you want to go. Making choices is like that. Choosing to believe another perception of a situation. Making them *your* choices, which puts you in a position to do something about whatever events follow. Refuse to be a victim, the only role left if we allow choices to be made for us. Choose to look at the consequences to your choices as things that you can manage. Learning to fly "on instruments" sets the stage for more opportunities to grow and live effectively.

## *Summary*

For all of us there are decisions to be made that range from the "no brainer" to those that intimidate. There is no question but that there is a category of decisions we ponder that affect the quality of our lives, that is often met with reluctance — we don't know what the outcome will be, we're not positive about what we want, we're not sure how to deal with the consequences, etc.

Something holds us short of moving toward that something that we want as a part of our lives. Identify that decision that sits in waiting, then make it, decide, as a concrete demonstration of a measurable step on this journey of deliberately managing your life.

# 8

# *The Freedom To Choose A Narrow Road*

I want to introduce what I believe to be an important underlying perception to our whole focus. When learning how to formulate perceptions that help us to live more effectively and efficiently, we must start with a new foundation. It is like reprogramming a computer to use a different operational system, and respond differently to the input it receives. The net result is that the input may be the same as before, but the output is entirely different.

Let's take a look at several specific areas in which this applies. The first has to do with a principle that gets little attention, but is crucial as a starting point to the process of learning how to process the day-to-day experiences, some of which are less than cooperative in making it easy to live like we want to.

It is common for most of us to struggle within the paradoxical uneasiness of restraint and freedom. The fixed and the flexible, the definitive and the undefined, challenge us to make decisions to form beliefs and choices. We can then elevate our existence from wandering to fulfillment. This is the difference between those who live effectively, and those who experience little of life beyond existing. The degree to which this process is a struggle or a pleasure, like everything else, depends on how we look at it. If we perceive anything that smacks of hard and fast and structured as restrictive, it will make those with a bent toward the unconventional less than comfortable. This life, under the silent mantra which mandates "Keep your options open!" is a reflection of a fear of a loss of personal power and control. It is reflective of a belief that everything must be directed from the get go, rather than a belief in the viability of managing some things as you go. It makes us neurotic, if we perceive concrete values and a committed direction eliminates personal flexibility and freedom. The truth is that this view actually inhibits the ability to achieve those valued states of living. We seem to have lost, or perhaps we never developed, a sense of integrating the value of commitment in relationship to the benefits of choosing from a value system reflecting freedom and flexibility. In other words, we seem to think that making a commitment interferes with choice. Structure and guidelines are seen as the antithesis to the idealism of the singing spirit of spontaneity.

Some time ago I met a very likeable man who unfortunately illustrates the point well. Having built a successful business, he enjoyed a comfortable lifestyle. He held the ticket most middle-aged men would love to have. Beautiful wife, new custom home, great cars and plenty of toys. One of the strengths of his personality was to believe that anything was possible. He was blessed with the capacity to visualize what could be accomplished, and get it put together. He didn't understand "No." It was simply an inconceivable response to what could be realized.

On the other hand, the idea of commitment had become aversive to him. It had come to be perceived as putting at risk the chance to experience all that life has to offer. He personified, "Keep your options open."

He was the kind of guy you hated to go out to lunch with. He oozed charm. His good looks caught the eye of the women all men secretly hoped would be looking at them with desire. Besides, they usually weren't shy about it with him. It made you feel invisible at the table. Occasionally, envy would rear its head. Self esteem suffers if you go out with a guy like this.

It was clear he didn't mind. It was also clear that he didn't understand something basic. Commitment is the agent that maintains what we tell ourselves is valuable. The underlying principle of commitment which makes it compatible with freedom, is that it is a freedom of choice issue, not an elimination of options.

The marital contract for example which includes fidelity, is not an externally imposed restriction of an existence without freedom. It is rather an expression of the freedom of choice. It is not depriving oneself of an opportunity to play around. It is rather an internally embraced protector of what at some point we have decided we will choose to make important to ourselves. It is a contract with ourselves to manage the emotional energy we have, and not allow it to be distracted to sabotage what is important to us.

The myth of "Keep your options open" ultimately cost this genuinely nice guy a marriage. His unconscious protest against the perceived restraints of commitment, kept him fighting with himself about not wanting to miss anything. Unfortunately, the theme becomes generalized in other areas as well. As might be expected he was also having financial problems.

He would make commitments that he fully intended to keep, but then something else would come up. The proverbial good deal, an interesting opportunity, or a chance to do something exciting. I don't know how many times I heard, "It's too good of a deal to pass up." The mythology here is that there will never again, in the course of life, be a deal that isn't as good or better. So he would redirect financial or emotional resources already committed toward something else, to more exciting or enticing opportunities.

I suppose someone could look at people like this and say that if they would just make some serious commitments, their lives would be less complicated. In actuality, people like this are probably more committed than the rest of us. His commitment, although unstated, was something like "I will do whatever it takes, to have what I want, when I want it, in the way I want it, regardless of cost." This is commitment! Our commitments need to be directed to enhance the quality and fulfillment of our lives, not to a continual stream of complications.

A balanced sense of commitment on the other hand says something different. It is to make a conscious choice to stay consistent, to be able to manage one's life in a way that doesn't jeopardize the things we want to hold as valuable. That isn't to say of course that there aren't any number of opportunities to get distracted.

Being a middle-aged American male, I have my own thing about what others may refer to pejoratively as "Big Boy Toys." That really isn't fair you know. It must be that testosterone enhanced perspectives are just hard to understand! In any event, my love for flying keeps an airplane on the top of the "Toy List." It is amazing however how many other things want to get on the list as well. Those new Harleys are sure nice, that twin engined off-shore racer is exciting, that cabin hidden away somewhere would be a great retreat to write and relax. On and on it goes.

The point is that big goals are easily compromised by little short term indulgences. I have watched many competent business and professional people undermine their goals by getting frustrated and impatient and grabbing an opportunity to feel better, but consequently delaying or destroying the ability to get the real goals accomplished. The issue here has nothing to do with a person's ability to get something done. It is rather undermined by unconscious perceptions.

It is not that difficult to set goals and form dreams when inspired. When however those things are superimposed on counter-productive perceptions, they will never be realized.

The point is that we all commit ourselves to something. If we are not clear about our existing perceptions, we will live them out, often with confusion about why things aren't coming together as we want, simply because we are living out the unconscious commitment to those perceptions.

Commitment is not a compromise of personal choice and freedom. It is a vehicle of accomplishment, recovery, preservation, gain, fulfillment and measurable progress into any area of life in which we wish to invest. I believe that we have evolved to a cultural philosophical position where we worship a new value.

This new value, is to have *no* permanent, irrefutable, absolute values. It is relativism to the nth degree. There is no doubt in my mind that we have moved away from the rigid legalism of guilt-inspiring judgment drawn from centuries of overbearing, patronizing rules that do nothing but keep people immature and irresponsible. We still cannot afford, however, to abandon the anchoring we need as a culture that only a clear and enforced set of values can provide.

To help unravel this, it is helpful to look at the apparent paradox of commitment and choice in a sequential fashion. In other words, choice is not prevented by commitment, it rather precedes it. Values are not the nemesis to freedom, but ultimately secure the privilege of choice.

People make commitments to loose weight, quit smoking or get in shape — but often for reasons that are stimulated by fear or shame.

If we are making commitments to something that is based on, let's say, a cultural value (hard bodies are better than soft ones), we will not be successful at maintaining whatever we achieve, because it is not *our* value.

I was consulting with a business client who had been trying to make a transition in her career. She had held a position for a number of years which had left her little time for her family, and less for herself. One day I had asked her how she would like her life to be. Actually, she had been complaining about how busy she was with her career, her children, and her other many commitments — all of which were certainly legitimate. She really had no answer to the question. I caught her off guard when I responded with, "You need to get a life." She simply sat across from me dumbfounded, blinked her eyes and had nothing to say. When we got around to talking about what she would really like her life to be like, she didn't have a clue beyond what her roles had been.

It became clear that her primary commitment had inadvertently become to live as a firefighter — just responding to one crisis and demand after another. She had unknowingly accepted a value that dictated an illegitimacy to placing anything other than crisis on the list of what was really important in life. There were plenty of legitimate needs in and around her life to demand her attention. Because she had absolutely no sense of how she really wanted to live her life, she had no life other than the obligations demanded by her circumstances. She was living by default.

As I began to help her get a focus on what would for her be a more balanced way to approach her life, she started to make choices to manage things differently. She was off to a good start. She invested some energy to determine what was true about herself. This included an accurate perception of her competency, fairness and specific capabilities. As she embraced those perceptions of herself, a significant shift began to take place. She had a foundation to stand on to make some life-acquiring choices.

Rather than being defensive and reticent, she began to move consistently with confidence toward what she wanted to accomplish. When she hit obstacles, she would stop and catch her breath, then get moving again. This process began because she captured a view of the "why?" to change, and made a commitment to process the events encountered in a way to keep her moving forward. One of the outcomes she identified was having a business in which her income was not dependent upon a political system which dictated every move she made. Further, it was to raise her income beyond the mediocre level she had been willing to settle for before. She identified outcomes for her business focus, the level of income and personal time.

Several months later I saw her again. She was depressed and exhausted. Earlier, she had in fact made some choices not to respond to every demand of her children, her business, etc., etc., but she succumbed. Why? She allowed herself to loose the picture of an outcome that was important enough to her. In other words, a clear picture of the kind of life she wanted to lead, to make it worthwhile to continue to perceive and process things differently on a day-to-day basis. She was seduced by the old perception: "What everybody else wants is the most important thing to satisfy."

Where she fell down was in beginning to reuse the old familiar perceptions to manage the reactions her world would predictably have to the changes she was making. What this means in concrete terms is managing views by managing thoughts. When an event happens, good, bad or otherwise, there is a spontaneous perception you will have of it. Any number of reasons will contribute to the way you see it. Our purpose is not to spend time trying to sort that all out. Occasionally that is necessary. Our purpose is to learn how to deal with those perceptions. Perhaps that is the genius behind refrigerator magnets. They hold the images of the things we wish to remind ourselves are important to keep or achieve.

We begin to see how the perceptions we have built on the thoughts we entertain either enhance or impair our success at what we are dealing with at the moment. The bottom line is that we have to have a clear commitment to what we want the outcome to be before we can make any sense out of trying to look at things differently.

Managing thoughts is absolutely the key. For this woman, her sincerity dictated that she consider every thought or view that came up about her choices. It paralyzed her. For example, when she had made plans to spend some time on a given day to work on developing her business, one of her children would get ill. Obviously, they needed her attention. The first thought that would enter her mind was, "Oh great, there goes this day. I will not get anything done." She would become resentful in her care taking of her child. She fell victim to the "either/or" perception of a dilemma. This "One way or the other" paradox left her with no choice but to be a "good mother," by abandoning one side of the opportunities of the day. The belief was "If you are going to be a good mother, you must put everything aside for your child." Not so!

This is where we learn to interject two things: a filter and an anchor. The filter says: "Any thought or perspective that does not allow me to keep moving, even at a modified pace and maintain my other commitments, must be edited out and given no time for consideration — period." This filter does not allow the presence of any perception of that immediate situation that implies no choices other than what is demanded of you.

The anchor is the commitment to finding a way to take care of necessary obligations and duties, and move toward what you want as well. This is an interesting perceptual challenge. Moving forward may mean a side step to the left, a dart to the right, a brief stop, a strategic retreat for the purpose of a modified direction. However, it never means looking at the situation of necessary adjustments as anything other than just that. It is the wise use of discretionary power to consider the issues, make choices and keep moving.

A "good mother" can attend to the needs of her children, and do something that fulfills the other things she wishes to do as well. I know this is sacred ground. Many good parents are concerned about their responsibilities of raising children. However, this is not a matter of devaluing or minimizing the validity of these concerns. It is rather a point about having a life that remains abundant with choices — including the one to devote exclusive time to parenting. Also, it retains the equally sacred choices to look at one's life and roles in a way that keeps the abundance of those choices available and realized.

Where the good mother struggled, was in not keeping her filter up and the anchor intact. Her heart drew her continually toward her children's needs. She allowed them to demand her total attention, while floundering about her personal objectives. She forgot to believe that she could balance, adjust and strategize her way through the maze of choices. Her perception was that there is something about choices that was translated into options of luxury, while she considered obligations to be those things which controlled her choices. These unconscious beliefs continually undid her efforts to maintain a focus on her outcomes, and develop new perceptions to help get there.

The challenge is to learn to develop a different way of perceiving to create a functional and working balance. In this sense, I believe in having your cake and eating it too. The necessary perception is that it is okay to consider the choices, and that integrating duty and desire can absolutely be done. We must make a commitment to that perception. That is the open door to unbelievable potential. It is here that we discover and realize those innate God-given gifts. This is where we exit the life of confusion about why things turn out the way they do. We no longer have to perpetually contribute to that unhappy outcome. We can, however, only accomplish this with the foundation of a commitment to those beliefs.

Another client demonstrates the other side of the coin. As an attorney, he was working for a law firm representing companies in a rather volatile industry. He had a professional reputation as being competent and capable. In spite of his success, he had some personal problems which kept paralyzing him from further personal or professional development.

He practiced in a professional environment that was anything but conducive to healthy perceptions. The administrative partner was a "hands on" manager of the firm and its legal staff. Translated, that means he was controlling, manipulative, controlling and more controlling. The subtle message that his management style communicated to his highly competent staff was, "Were it not for the directions, structure and watchfulness which I provide for this firm, none of you would do what you should, stay on top of things, serve our clients well, etc."

Although my client certainly believed himself to be far more than that (and he was — in spades), that kind of toxic environment had eventually put him back on his heels. Over time he did begin to wonder about himself, as a professional and a person. The environment had subtly kept him from developing personally and professionally. The problems he presented when he first came to my office were not feelings of poor self esteem or lack of self confidence, but rather symptoms of feeling terribly out of control of his own life.

What became clear as we identified some of the issues involved, was that he had a toxic way of perceiving things and processing his day-to-day experience particularly in his professional world. His perception of himself as a professional was of someone who was competent and capable in his field, but likely to do something to embarrass himself and therefore undermine his credibility and jeopardize his professional standing. Although this is an oversimplification of all the issues involved, this unconscious way of perceiving much of his experience in his professional arena made him a worried wreck.

What is amazing, is that in spite of the perceptual mess he was in, he performed extremely well. He represented his clients well, made well-received presentations to firms in his industry of expertise and at conventions of his peers. That fact further reinforces my contention that the reality of our experience is at times far less powerful than our perception of it and of ourselves. These perceptions will keep a person from enjoying success, experiencing a dream, and enjoying the life that he is a part of, by distorting them into something negative and incomplete.

As we went to work to help him deal with what was creating his malaise and confusion, several things became clear. First, he was able to recognize that he was in a toxic environment which was undermining his sense of direction. Second, he had sold out to someone else's idea of what he should and shouldn't be doing. Third, he had lost a sense of direction of his personal and professional life. He had embraced a perception of himself as someone who was probably going to do something stupid or embarrassing that would have extremely unwelcome consequences.

Through the course of working with him over several months, he became very clear on several issues which changed his approach to both his personal and professional life. His perceptions began to shift. He now began to see the firm he worked for differently. He didn't embrace the bad attitude of a maligned victim. Rather he began to see the tension being created by the supervisor of the particular office he worked in as doing him a great favor. This boss's determination for control and scrutiny over every minor detail of the practice shifted from a perception of a major irritation, to one of a significant favor.

The favor was inadvertent. The situation became so uncomfortable, so unresolvable, that it finally pushed my client to move past his own resistance to look at what his other professional options might be. As we talked, he was able to disclose thoughts which had been too uncomfortable to acknowledge. He wanted to have a business of his own.

The next step for my client was to get clear on the outcomes he wanted. To put is simply, he wanted a greater sense of freedom to exercise his own judgements on how to best manage his practice and his time. For him this was really a "rite of passage" into professional adulthood — to assume and manage direct responsibility for his career.

We frequently operate with a myth that suggests that the only truly important thing to get clear on is our goals. If however, we do not realize the necessity to manage our perceptions of our experiences while moving toward these goals, we will either fail or spend inordinate amounts of wasted energy trying to get to that end we have in mind.

It is exciting to see someone make significant perceptual shifts, learn how to sustain them and realize a new quality of life. For this man the issues were achieving freedom from a complete dependence on a controlling environment and developing a means for managing his life in a way that was more consistent with what he discovered he really wanted.

This kind of deliberate living excites me. Even though we cannot control the things that happen to us in the course of living, we can be deliberate about the direction we're taking. We do not need to live life by default. We can learn to mange problems and keep moving. I look at it this way — we're going to have problems anyway, even doing the things we don't want to do in life, so we might as well be going in the direction we want. It isn't going to cost us any more, and at least we get to create more of the life we want to experience.

A friend said something that is a good perception to attach to difficult circumstances. While struggling with some circumstances that will realistically continue to be present for another year, my friend said, "I am not going to miss the life that is to be lived now, in spite of what's going on, while I'm waiting for this to be over." Bravo!

The readily available perception for her was "Life will not feel good and be okay until this situation I'm dealing with is over." Because she had already made a commitment to use a filtering system for thoughts and views that lead her to other than where she wants to go, her negative perception of events to come was discarded before it had a chance to become operational. She, on the other hand, took an arbitrary leap of faith, and made a commitment to choose to perceive it differently. The choice: "I will live, enjoy my life, learn how to survive, thrive and manage this process, and when it is over, I will continue to do the same, enjoying the increased confidence in my ability to manage anything that may happen in my life." This was the use of her anchor.

I like to equate anchoring with commitment. It is not an externally enforced entity. Rather it is a deliberately embraced stabilizer. Commitments keep us on track.

Part of what I enjoy about my own personality is a diversity of interests, great enthusiasm for adventure and new challenges, projects, and things which stimulate my creative juices. I have a much deserved reputation in my family which is reflected in comments like: "What is he going to do next?" or "He never does anything except full speed ahead, or jump in all the way." The good-natured ribbing I receive carries with it a reminder of the pricking I get from the other side of that coin I know equally well—that the energy, creativity and drive I feel can be a restless curse. It has never been difficult for me to make commitments to things and follow them through to the end—sometimes the bitter end.

What has been more of an issue for me is the number of commitments to make. In my twenties and thirties, I was blessed with what, now especially, seems and enormous amount of energy to get things done. In my forties I have less of a reservoir to draw from. I approach things like I did when I was 25, but I run out of gas — still to my surprise — forgetting things aren't the same. I plan many projects I'll get done around home, horses and barn, and it doesn't happen like it used to.

Commitments benefit us because they at least keep us pointed in a general direction. Without an informed commitment little of value gets accomplished in our lives, nor does anything of worth last. I remember well a woman who would get inspired by the opportunity to do things that reflected what her dreams for a lifestyle were. For her it included a large home in a particular area, being married to the "right" type of person, and having the lifestyle of a woman who was loved and provided for well.

The picture from the outside was wonderful. A beautiful home, nice cars, a place for her animals, the choice to not have to work outside of the home, and the prestige of being married to a successful professional. She made a sincere commitment of her life to all of this. What she didn't realize was that she also made a commitment to all that goes with it as well.

That lifestyle was accompanied by significant mortgage payments. European cars often require expensive maintenance. All of the extra single purpose vehicles require licenses, insurance and maintenance. The large yard takes either a lot of time to maintain or the expense of hiring it done.

Her spouse was successful because of his willingness to invest time and energy to develop a career and then sustain it. She however perceived his ambition as an intimidating force, rather than the source of helping her to realize her dreams as well. For her not working, left her unproductive, isolated and eventually depressed. The sad outcome for her was the dissolution of everything she had dreamed of — not because it wasn't available to her; but because she had not informed herself realistically about what she had committed herself to. She wasn't prepared to deal with it, and was unwilling to allow her perceptions and choices about what was involved to reconcile themselves to her goals. She had unfortunately conflicting goals: a quality life style with no difficulties.

Her uninformed commitments became a strangulating presence. The price of involvement confused her. Had she understood more about commitment the "price-tags" would have been approached differently. Rather than having to deal with fear, blame and panic, it would have started the process of problem solving. Rather than, "I didn't bargain for this in the picture," it would have been, "What do we need to do to address the problems, and then move on."

The point again is that our perception of what we are dealing with contributes significantly to our responses to what may happen. Those perceptions are born out of what we know or believe. If we're committing to things with no more than inspiration or dreams, we are in deep trouble. Things happen — quoted somewhat more delicately than the famous bumper sticker!

Conversely — to realize that the ability to sustain movement toward a new level of performance or function must have an informed foundation, is to invest our energy well. If we start toward a goal with just inspiration, we only get distracted by the first of many things that quench our excitement. Fear of problems insists that these realities be ignored or minimized. "Oh, we'll cross that bridge when we come to it," can be a positive attitude to avoid getting bogged down in trivia. It can also be a reflection of an unwillingness to make informed decisions.

I have a friend I ride horses with who illustrates well another side of this posture. Some time ago he developed a product to be marketed through retail outlets selling home supplies. It required a manufacturing company to produce it to exacting specifications. While we were riding the other day, he told me that the first 3,000 units shipped to him, and 10,000 ready to be shipped to other outlets were completely out of the tolerances required.

It was interesting to reflect later on his attitude. It is very clear that he researched the need for his product well. He determined not only the need in general, but designed it in such a way as to give it a very unique market niche. His informed commitment to get this product on the market gave him an important foundation to deal with the current problem. He was not wasting time wondering if he should be undertaking this effort. He was not questioning his assessment of the market for his product. He was not questioning his judgement about taking on this venture. He was not doubting his communication skills to convey the required specifications to the manufacturer. He was not stalled.

His informed commitment allowed him to keep clearly focused on the only important issue: Either to get his manufacturer to deliver as agreed, or find one who will. His ability to stay clear and on track was the result of perceptions he developed to process normal problems. "I've done my homework, I know what I know, now I will perceive this as absolutely nothing more than a problem to be solved, so that I will keep moving toward what I have committed myself to do. No rethinking is allowed." That is his anchor for success.

This is not to say that he may well have days like the rest of us when the silent conversations with ourselves go something like: "What on earth ever possessed me to do this anyway?" That is only normal. What is important is that we don't stay there and get stalled. That is where the skill of filtering comes in. We must not listen to anything that will shift our perceptions of what we have made an informed commitment to, and jeopardize the outcome.

It takes commitment to get on course, stay there and sustain the results. I've watched many people make preliminary commitments, make a good start, perhaps even achieve their goal, then erode the accomplishment because their achievement was not based on an informed choice and their commitment was missing a willingness to learn how to effectively manage the surprises.

It is unfortunate that many bright, capable, talented, even gifted people never quite get to the point of enjoying the freedom of realized dreams. We get our appetites whetted; we get teased into enough experience to know that some result is possible, but then it mysteriously disappears and we often shrug and say, "Well it must not have been possible anyway," or "Maybe it just wasn't supposed to happen for me." This is the point of defeat, the lack of resolution I wish to warn about. "Don't stop before you begin! It's DANGEROUS thinking!" Some people work so hard, and get so close, then stop. It is almost as if they are afraid to believe that what they really want can happen for them.

The other day I came across a greeting card that had a large and majestic eagle pictured on the front. I appreciated the symbolism of eagles reflected in the inscription inside which read: "May you have the strength of eagles' wings, the faith and courage to fly to new heights, and the wisdom of the universe to carry you there."

Our perceptual framework does depend on these kinds of images, symbols and inspiration to keep us moving in the right direction. If we have those images, or anchors, they will stabilize and sustain any new course of direction.

A patient who is recovering from a major illness or trauma needs to have an image beyond hospital beds, concerned health care providers, IV tubes and immobilization. That picture offers nothing to encourage recovery. There must be a new picture formed to perceive the daily drudgery as something, that leaves no question as to the outcome. Find for yourself an image, a picture, something that represents the outcome for you in living successfully, and keep it where it will constantly remind you of where you're going.

I saw a television newsmagazine report some time ago about a young woman who had sustained some very serious injuries as a professional stunt woman. As her family was thrust into an active role to make decisions about the care their daughter would receive, they made some insightful decisions. The young woman's condition was grave, the prognosis was less than optimistic.

Knowing exactly how their daughter would approach the situation — full speed ahead toward full recovery — they made sure that she was in the care of professionals who would give her the necessary mental space and encouragement. Their statement in this report reflected how they had moved her out of care facilities that did not support her ambition and perceptions for her recovery. No one was denying the seriousness of her condition or that some effects of her injuries may remain. They just refused to have her in an environment that had perceptions of her recovery potential as less than what their daughter would strive for. The point is that they made a commitment to an unwavering position: "We will support her vision, her ambition, her perceptions of how she will deal with this." This is learning to let someone else's eagle fly. They made sure that her environment would do the same.

The business person trying to expand or develop a business needs a picture of something other than cash flow struggles, payables, slow receivables and regular discouragements. They do not need a commitment to pie in the sky, but rather a picture of their role and the outcome they want. They need the pictured image of something that represents the end result that nurtures and sustains the daily activity toward that goal. It is not enough to have a goal. It is essential to have that goal matched to a working perceptual system that looks past the day-to-day struggles, and allows forward movement.

For example, the business person can look at daily problems as continued obstacles, keeping him from his goal. Or, he can choose to look at each of those problems as a check list of things to get resolved and therefore out of the way, leading him one increment closer to what he wants. Commitment to a specific way of perceiving what happens to us in anything, is crucial to the quality of our lives. The perception that says, "There is a way to get this problem resolved" creates the foundation for that fact to be realized. Rather than getting lost or distracted in what is happening, we should keep looking for the answer through our own creativity, or from the network of those around us who can provide concrete ideas. The commitment to a problem-solving perception is the essential difference.

Lately, I have had a number of clients who are parents involved in the most difficult stage of raising children — that usually awful time called adolescence. I had one mother recently share her agony over her son. His latest report card was a parent's nightmare. His choices of late had resulted in an arrest for being a minor in possession of alcohol. Mom was feeling, and rightly so, the inability to be of much of an influence in her son's choices. Her perception was that he was putting his entire future at risk, and therefore would not experience the quality of life that she hoped for him to have. Consequently, she was depressed, worried, angry and guilty.

In talking about how she was dealing with the problem, I shared some optional perceptions that she could use to overlay what she had to watch her son go through.

Perception number one: his behavior was a compliment to her. She had done such an appropriate job in raising him, he was now doing exactly what he should be doing as a normal adolescent; he was starting the learning process of direct consequences for the choices he was making independent of her. Her role was now shifting to consultative parenting, that is walking through this with him, not as a director, but someone to give him tools to deal with the consequences of his choices.

Perception number two: He needed to be going through this now. If he were being the "perfect" son now, he would most likely do some of this craziness when he was in his twenties or thirties. The consequences then are far more severe when he has his own career, and perhaps a marriage and a family at risk.

Perception number three: The pain she felt for him was okay. She should see her role differently now than she has known it to be. This is a difficult shift in parenting. If we embrace new perceptions of our roles however, everyone stays healthier, and the eventual outcome is more what we want. Everyone operates with that important foundation for mental and emotional health — clarity on who is responsible for what.

Relinquishing the dream, whether to recover as much as possible from an illness or injury, have a successful business, or raise good kids, because it was "too big for me," is certainly not a conscious process for most people. The challenge comes and we think we won't be able to measure up. Or, the old perceptual system kicks in, and undermines somethings that in reality can be realized. So we close the curtain on their hope. We don't understand that dreams happen when you follow the rules. And commitment has a few rules.

First, you must make an informed choice. Inspiration is certainly a part of that. However, you cannot successfully commit to anything without knowing the end and the price. The price is irrelevant as long as we accept that there will be one, and that the return is significant enough for us.

Second, make a commitment to accomplish the choice and give it the status of a sacred decision. It cannot come up for review — maybe modification, but not reconsideration.

Third, enlist the cooperation of a trusted witness, someone to help keep you on track. These are people who have demonstrated their own beliefs and abilities about perceiving life in such a way as to get from the normal and basic, to the inspired and rewarded.

Fourth, eliminate negative words in your vocabulary: "Can't" is a good place to start. It may seem trite to not use certain words, but remember that your subconscious believes everything you tell it.

Fifth, get familiar with some new vocabulary: "Can" and "Will" are wonderful facilitators of commitment. This is not just a lot of positivistic self cheerleading. It is using words that are consistent with the perceptions about your situation that will enhance your ability to get to the realization of what you want to achieve.

Sixth, never say die. It is okay to get tired and discouraged. What is important is what you do about it. Catch your breath, sigh if you have to. Then get moving, even slowly if necessary.

Seventh, create a perception, a label you will put on the picture of every event from start to finish. It may just be something that says, "Well, this must be part of what comes with the territory," or "Surprises don't mean I have to give up." Anything is good that will allow you to put the events in a pigeon hole, contain them, so you can keep moving.

I am painfully aware that what I have written does not represent all of the truth about perceptions and commitment. But I am joyfully aware that if you embrace these seven simple rules you can make absolutely revolutionary changes take place in your life.

Progress toward the goal of commitment is important in terms of how it's measured. If we can see measurable movement, then we're okay. When clients and I are working through difficult issues their sense of progress is often clouded by emotional turmoil. As an outside observer, I have the luxury of watching their recovery, healing or progress. They are moving, and I know the end result of their movement—a destination already identified and determined by the direction they are pointed.

Their view is often different however. From the inside of these experiences the emotional swings do not easily allow a clear view. It is something like the vibration-distorted view I used to have as a kid, racing down the hills on a primitive self-made soap box derby-type coaster, on hard rubber tires, with no suspension. Between the vibration and the tears from the wind in my eyes, about all I could do was point the contraption in the right direction when I started, and hope I landed somewhere near where I had pointed it.

Some time ago I read an interesting magazine interview with a local utilities company president that illustrated this principle. He was asked what he believed to be the greatest challenges facing his company over the next twenty years. I fully expected him to comment on the need for conservation or the development of additional sources of power for our growing region. What he did say, surprised and delighted me: "The greatest challenge facing us is to equip our people to be adaptable and resilient to a continually changing environment."

Cheers for a refreshing insight from the corporate top!

In the context of our focus on commitment what the executive said contains a gem of great value. It should be expected that things may change at any moment. A trend in our business, a shift in a relationship, an injury or accident can confront us with choices.

When things get confusing, and they seem to in a way commensurate with the size of the goal, we sometimes have to go back to the most basic commitment. It is not "What am I going to do now?" but "Who will I be?" If we are clear on that, we will *never* be at a loss about what to do. Other commitments may have variables we can't control. You lose a limb to cancer and you can't run that marathon. Your spouse leaves you and you have no relationship to invest your love in any longer. Any number of circumstances can raise their ugly heads. What do we do?

It is absolutely consistent with the idea of commitment, to readjust, refocus, redirect the energy, but in a modified form. We just cannot make some things happen. A commitment to wisdom and prudence suggests that at times we need to move in directions other than our original plan. That is not an embarrassment. It is a demonstration of prudence, integrity, survival, and the ability to capitalize on what happens. A commitment to integrity is to maintain a grip on the goal, but take the time needed to reevaluate the strategies necessary to continue. I believe it is a greater glory to overcome, than to flow with an easy process. It is the foolhardy who keep going at all costs, and fail to recognize the signs.

A number of years ago while practicing in southern California, I had clients who were in the entertainment industry. I remember one young woman who desperately wanted to be a "star" in movies and television. She was delightful, ambitious, and dedicated to her goal. She had been "working" at it for several years. By the time I saw her as a client she was depressed, discouraged and broke.

As we reviewed her past several years, she certainly demonstrated a commitment, at least as far as being tenacious. What she had not looked at was that her methodology wasn't working. Unfortunately, she had her goal and her method so intimately tied together that she was going nowhere but into a deeper depression.

Her methodology was undesigned and by default. It went something like, get an agent, submit a portfolio, buy an answering machine, hope for the best, and have no other commitments (i.e. jobs), to get in the way of what *might* happen. Consequently, she had a great deal of time on her hands while she lived for the phone to ring. She did little to demonstrate to herself any expertise in her life, so her depression focused on the fact, among others, that she wasn't good at anything but being idle. She certainly demonstrated commitment however. Unfortunately, it was to something that wasn't coming close to working.

There was none-the-less, still value for her in this "unproductive" cycle. It was better to hope for achieving great success while doing little to actively pursue it, than giving it everything she had and risk failing. At least failing in the system she had designed could be blamed on other factors — lousy agent, no good parts, etc. The truth is, she actually had what she wanted, and was committed to maintaining it. This was the "glory" of being an aspiring actress, living a "hoped for" life fed by dreams and possibilities, and unconsciously not having to live with the added stress of achieving and maintaining the kind of success she wanted.

She had a difficult time looking at all of this, because it meant change. Not change to the dream, but change to the methods of getting there, and then committing to that as much as the dream itself.

It takes maturity to distinguish the difference between the impossible and an enormous challenge. We're often too close to it ourselves to know. Maturity asks the objective and informed for advice. The immature ask no one and blindly run on, or away. Either direction results in the tragedy of not experiencing the joy of a redirect, or the emotionally economical choice of cutting losses, and reinvesting in something more productive.

As parents, our children need the demonstrated perspective of effective living as defined by resiliency, not perfect choices, the control of all decisions, and the myth that if you do things just right everything will turn out okay. We can do every thing okay on the way to the poorhouse. Those same children, colleagues, or whoever benefit from the demonstrated perspective, that there are *always* choices to do something, and not be a victim of events. Our choices here seem to be folding, denial, or commitment to this belief. This is one of the most important foundational perceptions to process everything with. In other words, it doesn't matter what happens. We cannot afford to allow events to dictate the ultimate outcome of anything. This is not to deny the often major impact that any event may have on us. It is however to refuse to allow it to control any aspect of our lives, particularly the ultimate outcome.

A commitment to a belief is the most secure and centering thing we can do. It becomes a pivotal point around which everything else revolves and is given limits.

About 25 years ago a college friend of mine got married. He

decided that it would be great to honeymoon in the San Juan Islands, one of the treasures of our beautiful Northwest. He rented a motor yacht and with his new bride headed north. The approximately 100-mile trip to the islands nestled in the inland waters between Washington State and British Columbia, was uneventful. Their arrival in the San Juans presented many opportunities for exploring, beach combing, and whatever else honeymooning couples might wish to do. One day they decided to head ashore at a remote island. After anchoring the boat in a protected bay, the dingy was launched and off to shore they went. They got much more than they anticipated.

Not being a particularly savvy seaman when my friend dropped anchor, he thought that the best way to secure the boat was to pull the anchor line tight, tie it off, and all would be well. Not so! He had forgotten the tides.

About four hours after dropping anchor and going ashore, the honeymooners returned to their beached dingy only to discover the cruiser had disappeared. Following a frantic launch of the dingy they spotted the cruiser a couple of miles away drifting lazily on the receding tide. The incoming high tide lifted the anchor and floated the boat away from the island.

You can adapt the idea of commitment to anchoring. We have to reconcile ourselves to the fact that we have to leave some slack in the anchor line (expectations and plans), so that we have some means to adjust to the circumstances which will always be changing.

Risk-taking is what gives us the experience to become familiar with the nature of change and the need to accept it as simply a part of the commitment process. Security is not found in a rigid, inflexible position. It is in knowing that things do change and you can't always control that. What you can control is how far they will go, and what you will do in response to any or all changes. We can only relax and be comfortable if we believe that what is happening is normal and okay. If our experience is outside of that belief, we become dis-eased. Not because of the event, but because of what we believe. If things go wrong, it is okay. If things are confusing, it is okay. If you don't know what to do, that's okay — just keep looking for answers, don't reevaluate the decisions.

It is possible to develop the same level of comfort and ease with perspectives that are absolutely insane, and feel entirely at home within that view. I saw a recent interview on a national television news magazine of a Neo-Nazi leader in western Europe. It was actually chilling to watch him, with a placid expression, describe the need to still purge the Fatherland of the rat-like pestilence represented by "the Jews and other foreign waste." There was no concept for him of why the rest of the civilized world stood in opposition to his perspective. For him it was absolutely true, ethical, moral and able to stand the scrutiny of God himself. He was committed to a perspective that gave him purpose, direction, filtered out alternative views and gave him no cause to reconsider.

The point is that commitment, be it based on true or distorted reality, is the foundation and guarantor of an outcome representative of the beliefs which stimulate it. If you want to get somewhere or accomplish something of importance, make an informed choice and make a commitment. Then if you are falling short of what you want to be achieving or experiencing in your life, it is not the end result of having no commitment. Rather there are other, often unconscious commitments at play, which are antithetical to, or stand in the way of whatever new direction you may want to go.

It doesn't take long to discover an inner tug-of-war. I read a piece of research recently having to do with careers and levels of income associated with them. One point was made very clearly: if you want to make over $35,000 per year, EXPECT stress and hassles. It is entirely possible that we can mismatch our commitments, and therefore set ourselves up to be confused over the lack of expected results in ourselves or our situations.

I do not intend to imply at this point that a talented and focused person cannot accomplish meaningful goals, financial or other, and also live a balanced life with the ability to manage the stress and strain that goes with it. On the other hand, we cannot manage something we're not aware is occurring. If we want to tackle those goals that stretch us beyond the limits of our present comfort zone, we will get stretched. Stretching brings a certain level of discomfort.

The person with an informed commitment, knowing some of the realities to expect, sets the stage for a resolve he can live with. Uninformed commitments leave us prematurely invested in things that often have either high price tags, or surprises that set us back on our heels. One of the sad things that happens is that people get confused over their own reactions, misperceiving themselves as not having perseverance, or drive, when it is really just a matter of not being prepared. I am guilty at times of wondering why I occasionally seem so unmotivated. I forget how much energy I expend on the many things I always have going on, which result in being exhausted. It used to make me nervous when I ran out of gas. I got worried that the level of energy I enjoy working with was gone.

What I have learned, and has become a new way of perceiving a day on the couch, is this: I am tired, it must mean that I have spent more emotional dollars than I've earned lately. If I will rest and just putz around, I will make an emotional energy deposit and I will spontaneously get going when I have the reserve to do so. This involves learning the truth about something over time, then trusting in it.

It is interesting how much emotional and physical energy is spent in protest, fighting the unpleasant or unexpected complications of a choice or decision. As we engage in protest, our energy which is completely capable of enduring, managing or solving problems is spent. We have little if nothing left with which to problem-solve, cope or manage the situation. Perhaps we protest because we believe at least we can do *that,* if nothing else, to respond. The perspective I want to inject is that there is a great deal more we can do. If we waste all of our energy in protest, we never discover the resources we possess to problem-solve, therefore, become a believer in dropping the protest, and getting on with solving it.

Imperative words like, should, ought, must, have to, cannot, are toxic and dangerous to any process of change. They are the singularly most effective carcinogenic substance to eat away at change and growth. These words refocus the normal events in any great undertaking into a nasty and unwelcome, impossibly uncomfortable, and entirely unnecessary development. If I have learned anything by this mid-point in my life it is the beneficial necessity of the unexpected. These events, as truly unpleasant as they are, are not created by anyone or anything for our intended discomfort; they remain as beneficial springboards to the development of functional abilities to new levels of performance.

Believe me, I do wish there were another way. I would like to believe I am smart enough to know what needs to be done, and just do it. I've discovered that I am thoroughly human—I don't change or stretch until I have to. A healthier response than protest to the unwelcomed is acceptance. Acceptance does not imply consent. I don't have to like it or agree with it to be accepting. Acceptance is the deliberate embracing of an event to rob it of its power to steal our energy to manage or deal with it. It is a matter of personal choice to willfully involve ourselves in anything — particularly unpleasant things. This is a crucial perception to allow us to process and manage anything that happens. It is imperative to do this — it is the only perception that allows us to process events and continue to make progress to what we want to experience in our life. It is the great antidote to victimization.

We talked earlier about the necessity behind behaviors and choices that people make. Whether or not those necessities make any sense to us is totally irrelevant. The frightening thing for moms, dads, friends, coaches, physicians, and leaders in any situation is that we have no control of the other person's choice. We do however have an enormous amount of power in an entirely different way. Commitment to what we will be in the process is vitally important. Parents sometimes need to shift to being consultants, rather than directors. Employers need to be listeners, not autocrats. Physicians need to tell people what choices they have and give them the tools to exercise them, not tell what is or is not going to happen. As we shift our role, it empowers the other person to no longer resist his responsibility and choices. When resistance is no longer necessary, a creative process of change can begin. Otherwise, it is absolutely paralyzed.

Try this task for the next 30 days. Make a specific and measurable decision to do something that you have wanted to get done. This can be something you have already attempted, or perhaps just been thinking about. Before you begin, decide two things: first, how you will choose to look at challenges to this goal — define them ahead of time; second, decide who you will be curing this process. In other words, visualize your response to the progress and problems in a way that will keep you on a committed direction toward what you want to achieve.

## *Summary*

Take a look at one area in which the lack of a clear decision or commitment is preventing you from accomplishing what you want. Decide what commitment you will make, set an exact date, day, and time when you will begin. Be fair and realistic. Secondly, find something to symbolize that decision and keep it conspicuously around for the next six months.

# 9

# *A Perspective On Values*

It has become clear to me that one of the many sources of stress and dis-ease that humans experience comes from living in a manner that is inconsistent with our conscious and unconscious values. The net result is a confusing and distressing experience. The things which we want to happen don't, and the things we don't want to happen do, often to our bewilderment. We could paraphrase Apostle Paul's frustration and occasional self disgust which goes something like: "The things I wish I did I don't, and the things I wish I wouldn't do, I do."

It is difficult enough when we are clear on our values, appreciate their importance, and have a commitment to demonstrate them. When we are not clear, whether through indifference, lack of awareness, or an absence of understanding of how important values are, we are absolutely lost. By that I mean that we inadvertently give ourselves up to a fatalistic system of living by default — "Whatever happens will happen." If we have doubts about our already established values, we are inevitably drawn into a life experience that ricochets between unsubstantial icons and ideals, and good intention and self preservation.

I consider myself what I would call a "Recovering Fundamentalist." Having been raised in a home environment that strictly enforced the rules and regulations of a legalistic conservative Christianity, I was real clear about the way things, and I, should be. Being the determined independent individual that I have always been, I just learned to exercise my own definition of how to live within that system. The result however was also living with unnecessary guilt and a fear of discovery. What is interesting in retrospect is that I didn't really do anything wrong as far as what I understand moral law to be — it was just that my internally embraced (good) values, were simply demonstrated differently than the letter of the fundamentalistic law. This created internal conflict demonstrated in a number of ways.

It required that I learn to speak the rhetoric of the church community I was a part of, but live in a way that was conscientiously all right, but to the edge or the outside of that system's sacred norms. On the one hand, I have always enjoyed being a paradox, causing confusion to static systems. However, the price tag was a lingering uncertainty about my place within that system, and the precariousness of having good values, but living in a system that expected a different demonstration of them.

For example, some of the basic tenants of faith include such things as humility, satisfaction with one's place in life, and dying to one's self. I have always been a forward-moving, driven, ambitious, less-than-meek entrepreneur at heart, which created often confusing dilemmas. Not given to waiting for things to happen, the system of values I was a part of, which implied that one should let God take care of things — especially the direction of your life — drove me absolutely nuts. I would try to be patient, follow some kind of a nebulous response to a vague "leading," only to feel quite spastic.

My real value system believed that I had been given gifts and talents which longed to be exercised, as well as dreams and ambitions to accomplish. The external value system of the community I was a part of implied that that was only an expression of one's self, basically sinful and to be denied — the old "death to self" routine.

I finally realized after years of living in this conflict of inner and outer values, that I had to extricate myself from the system that countered everything I was wired to do with those well-established inner values. It was a kind of mutiny as viewed by those in the system. I was approached with expressions of great concern and fear for my spiritual well-being by those who were deeply entrenched in that system. What they could not hear, was that I was full of faith, hope and love and would express that in a way different from their perceptions of the norm.

We're not talking about anything bizarre here. Just basic things like taking direct charge and responsibility for one's life. Deciding what you want to do, and then setting your heart to it with all of the energy and gifts God gives you to use. It certainly acknowledges the source of the creative energy and giftedness, but doesn't get bogged down in the paralysis of what the heart and spirit are stimulated to do, and what a particular community dictates should be the form of expression.

A number of years ago now, Amy Grant came on the scene and rose to prominence as a gospel recording artist. This talented young woman touched thousands of people with her beautiful voice, personality of warmth and message of hope. She became a star of the Christian community and was THE Christian recording artist. Then something happened. Amy made a choice, which was perceived as, "She went secular."

From the sidelines as an interested observer of what happens when someone makes choices that create change, I saw that she took a lot of heat. What always amazes me is that as a body of people who call ourselves "Christian," that is, like Christ, we often fail miserably at demonstrating basic values, particularly those of unconditional love (I Cor. 13). The perceptions of her were based on an unspoken belief that suggests that if you are a good Christian, you don't waste your talents in secular singing, you don't go out and become a part of that world, be thankful for what God has given you, and leave well enough alone.

The point I am making is that we all have internally-embraced values. Some we are clear on, others we are not. Beyond becoming clear on what they are, we need to make sure that we integrate these inner values with a lifestyle that is consistent with them. If we don't do that, we create an inability to process the day-to-day issues that come up, and get past them to some proactive resolution. We waste our energy with a conflict between the inner and the outer values agenda which has a great deal of influence on the direction of our lives.

One of the themes that certainly comes up often in my office is focused on that conflict, and how to get free from it. I have seen one client on and off over the years who illustrates well the conflict and the freedom. This young man originally came to me as the result of a referral from his physician. He was depressed and highly anxious. He had been injured on the job and was on a disability leave. It was highly probable that he would never return to his former type of employment. The obvious issues at hand included the loss of income, how to support his family, and what to do about his health and his future.

The early focus of intervention was to help him manage these crises and get some degree of control over his life. Thankfully, over time he did a remarkable job of redirecting his energy. He started a business of his own, and became the envy of many of his friends who watched him generate income above and beyond what he had made in his pervious career. He developed some of the perceptual tools we're talking about, and completely redirected his life. He said to me one day, "Losing my job was the best thing that ever happened to me — it forced me to change."

That was phase one for him. Phase two, which illustrates the point we're discussing on values, started several years later. He called the office one day in a panic. He and his wife were separated, there were allegations against him of domestic violence, things were a horrendous mess.

To put it simply, this man was a terminal nice guy. He bent over backward to please everyone, and would do anything to avert disappointment or displeasure. In his new business, he sold a lot of recreational equipment. If someone was unhappy with a purchase, he would go so far as to buy it back, sometimes at a loss to himself, just to keep the customer from being unhappy with him. Within his family system which included his wife, children and very involved in-laws, he had a well-defined role. It went something like, "If there is a problem, you should take responsibility for it; if someone gets angry about something, it is up to you to fix the problem, and above all, never express how you feel about what goes on within this family." To put it bluntly, he was the designated jerk/scapegoat of the family. The message was "you're stupid, and we expect you to act like it." He usually did.

The conflict of values came in at this point. His inner values were to be nice, helpful and never make waves. The outer values as defined by the system he was a part of dictated that he never take a stand against the system, and accept whatever it said to him with absolutely no self-preserving interest. The present crisis found him under scrutiny by the police who had been told by "the system" that he was an unfit father, an abusive spouse, had no concern for his children, and wouldn't let his frustrated wife leave the house during the conflict they were engaged in.

He was fit to be tied. The legal system had him by the throat with serious allegations. If he didn't defend himself, he was toast. The family system had him too. He was not to fight back, he was to accept their judgement, and not identify where the real responsibility should be focused. This is the double-bind of conflicting value systems — damned if you do and damned if you don't.

Literally, his survival and sanity depended on violating one of the value systems. He either had to quit "Be nice and roll over," or "Never stand up and confront the truth." He was deeply invested in both.

He chose, with much angst, to confront the latter. In doing so, he unleashed the wrath of a scorned system. It was really amazing to watch things unfold from the sidelines. As he took a leap of faith to embrace only one value system, everyone, from his in-laws, to his wife, and even his children got into the act.

Remember, this is a man with a heart of gold. Often tactless and insensitive, yet he has a spirit about him that draws admiration. The only way he could break out of this terribly dysfunctional system was to grab onto a new perception of himself. It went something like, "I am a decent person who wants to do what is right, and who deserves to be treated with respect." It was interesting to watch him struggle with that. He had accumulated little evidence to support that perception of himself. The family system made sure he had none.

As he stepped outside of the role the "system" had defined for him, some profound changes began to take place. His daughter said to her mother one day, "Mommy, has Daddy gotten taller?" He was literally standing up straighter. As he stopped playing out the old role of defending every thought and feeling he had, several shifts took place. His wife, who played a very dominant and manipulative role in their relationship, who up to this point "couldn't trust him," (read *wouldn't*), became confused, angry and depressed. He was no longer in a position to be controlled by the family's rules and expectations. Her problem was now having to learn how to relate to him in a different role, this time a healthy one. Rather than taking full responsibility for the well being of the relationship, he was now allowing her to carry her share — if the relationship was going to work and be healthy, she had to participate in the function of problem-solving and the maintenance of intimacy as well.

She was livid; he was scared. As in all systems, values included, they will exert enormous effort to bring things back to homeostasis — return to normal. Being the one who stimulates that kind of change is hard duty. Maintaining the new posture with different perceptions about oneself in a situation is difficult. The good news is that things do finally restabilize, if we tenaciously hold to that new perceptual value system.

In his case, he has. His marriage is significantly different. It still has problems, but it's now a partnership, not a parent/child structure. He has greater respect from his children, not because he went to war with the system, but because he is less scattered because the inner war of conflicting values is over. In other words, he is free to express his feelings to his children, discipline them, direct them as necessary and not hear about it from "the system." He would historically have been angry at the system, but of course couldn't express that, so the children would take the heat having done the "do you know what Daddy did" reporting to the system. The in-laws are in a different position. They are now included in the family by invitation, not the historical invasion on every issue. It takes energy to maintain a newly-defined system, but it certainly takes less energy than surviving with the old one. This entire shift could only take place because of new perceptions.

So much of the trouble I see people have in their lives, whether like this man in his family, or someone else in his business or profession, is self-inflicted by perceptions we have of our circumstances, and a belief that we cannot change them. I believe in prayer, but most of the time we're just asking God to fix the problems we've created, and then keep on repeating. We need to learn how to get out of our own way. Learning new perceptual tools is a key ingredient. If we're going to pray, let's ask God to help us keep our eyes open.

Three decades ago, we watched an established value structure in our culture give way to free love and antiestablishmentarianism. From the ensuing chaos came a call for a return to predictable norms. Then came the silent majority, followed by the moral majority with its fundamentalistic fervor. We went from assumed benefits to rules and regulations, from strict and even rigid values, to uncertainty about the role of values, if any.

We have now come to a place of cultural insanity, where the value of freedom of expression has perverted itself into out-of-control crime. We need to reintroduce a sane set of values in our culture, and be willing to enforce the necessity of them. There is right and there is wrong. Ambiguity is not a value, it is a loophole intended for freedom, but destined for aimlessness.

While it is not my intention to explore upheaval and broad social values in this book, understanding what changes have meant to us in a short period—how they have created personal uncertainty in people—is fundamental to an understanding of how we perceive ourselves and the world around us.

How can we be sure of the probity of our values during any period of social history? How can we measure them on a scale of goodness and personal effectiveness? I believe in the test of pragmatism: "Is it working?" If it is not working there is something wrong at the values base, either with balance or compatibility. The test of pragmatism, however, does not infer license or freedom to act outside of social norms.

The statement, "No pain, no gain," reflects a typical conflict of values. We may want measurable progress in an area of importance to ourselves. We have thought it through, assessed its benefit and know that it will bring us pleasure and satisfaction. On the other hand, all of us possess values of self preservation and pain avoidance. Until we deal with the second set of values, sometimes deeply ingrained, we will never accomplish the new objectives. In other words, our self-preservation value will overshadow the accomplishment value. It is not just a matter of getting pumped up and motivated. Nor can we just discard the values of self-preservation and pain avoidance. We must rather find a different way to look at it. The perspective must be developed and embraced, and consistently held on to. And pain often is the necessary filter through which values must be strained. As a filter, pain becomes a reminder of achievement rather than a threat from which we retreat.

I know when I'm riding my horse correctly, my calves hurt the next day. When riding English, part of the position in the saddle is having your feet in a vertical line position from your shoulder, and your heels down. If you're a "cool" rider they're way down. Because I don't ride every day, my calves don't stay stretched like they should. My pain is nonetheless a measurement of doing it right.

To use pain as a reminder is to say, "Every time I feel this pain, it tells me that I am on track toward my goal. It is the yardstick of accomplishment, a measurement of my forward progress." Every step up in any worthwhile endeavor is accompanied by discomfort. It is the triumph of breaking through the discomfort that gives us a high.

I think it is worth restating that pain, or the consequence of stepping into new unfamiliar territory, can become the encouraging reminder of progress undertaken rather than a warning sign of approaching danger or discomfort. Discomfort is translated from warning into a vehicle by which we measure and monitor the progress being made. An athlete compares after-exercise heart and respiration rates from one exercise period to another; system stress is measured against system stress. It is one of the important ways of measuring conditioning. Physical conditioning is not accurately measured at rest. Nor is it measured when looking your best. After a great performance most athletes look tired, some exhausted, all sweaty and unglamorous. Some even collapse after giving the sum total of their conditioned bodies for an event.

To deal with conflicting values is not a matter of discarding one or the other, nor deciding that values are too restrictive. It is rather a matter of redefining them in a way that they can actually compliment each other. An example could be the different personalities in a relationship. Common sense would seem to indicate that the more two people are alike, the more compatible they should be and the more trouble-free their relationship. But this seldom holds true.

The likelihood of two people getting along well in a close relationship is probably more dependent on their dissimilarities than their similarities. Those who are alike are often in conflict over things like power, control and leadership. Dissimilarities set the stage for conflict as well, but also provide a wonderful opportunity for complementing one another. Any relationship that is without conflict is headed for trouble.

A few years ago I ran across some research that indicated that the level of intimacy in a relationship was dependent on the quality of the problem-solving skills of the couple. It could be said as well that conflict and problem-solving are necessary ingredients in the establishment and maintenance of intimacy. To be candid, I wish this weren't true — I don't like conflict. My own myths about relationships have included a desire for a conflict-free state of relational existence. Fortunately, I long ago realized that it didn't quite work that way.

Once we have taken the risk to dream, and then plan for the fulfillment of that dream, we must take a look at the values we operate with because they will enhance or inhibit our success. An amazing amount of the clinical work I do revolves around a few central themes. One of those is helping people get out of their own way and from shooting themselves in the foot. Human nature gives those of us in the mental health fields great job security. Somebody is always in trouble. We're always doing something to inhibit ourselves, our relationships, businesses, friendships, children, goals and dreams. There's not much we don't foul up at times.

You'd also think that those of us in this field would learn from other people's mistakes and not make them ourselves—draw your own conclusions about that one! It doesn't seem that it should be so difficult to chew gum and walk at the same time—to serve people and to avoid the mistakes they make. Some female friends of mine consider that observation to be a "guy" thing, and say we're only human.

The failure to value the nature of the human condition is expensive. To set ambitious goals outside the reach of your personal limits is a set up for disappointment. Like many entrepreneurial types, I like the exhilaration of excitement-fed energy bursts of activity. It's fun and inspiring to be able to get a lot of work done in a short amount of time. Several years ago, in a six-month period, I expanded and moved my local office to a new location, established a satellite office, remodeled the kitchen in my home, added a dining area, and refurbished my twin-engined airplane in and out. The former values which drove me to overdo don't serve me well any more.

One of those old values I had to let go of was the return I received from doing all of these things myself. I have replaced it with a new value: Checkbooks are for projects. I can't describe the joy it gives me these days to watch someone else work on my home. To be truthful that was a difficult one to let go of. Between the good old Protestant work ethic, and my sense of measurable accomplishment from these things, letting go came hard. I have remained active with some projects, but keep them at a level for my mid-forties energy level and consistent with the other things I want to preserve energy for that bring benefits to my life.

My swan song of projects was my new stable built a few years ago. I get enormous satisfaction from its efficiency, how well it helps me care for my animals and the way it enhances my home and property. One of the reasons I can enjoy the value of it is the redistribution of other values. Rather than getting my enjoyment from just building things myself it has been time to focus measurable accomplishments on things that still allow me to enjoy the lifestyle I have worked hard to create. In other words, I modified the value of hands-on work.

What we can't afford to discard or modify are the absolute values of morality and ethics which give our lives and society form and function. We must, however, learn to weigh and adjust those values which serve us well at one point in time, but inhibit and frustrate us elsewhere at another. It is safe to assume that whenever we add a new value to our internal operating system, an old one must be also discarded. If we're going to start a new business, then for a while we will need to modify the expectation of comfort. To undertake a goal of personal development will likely change relationships around us — so be prepared. Again, personal change does not necessitate a major disruption or termination of significant relationships. They will need to go through a period of adjustment and change, otherwise they will impair or obliterate the personal goal for new directions.

Values serve us well. There need to be those which never change; they are bedrock. There need to be those values which change occasionally to serve us in the pilgrimage of growth. There are values we carry with us which have never been our own and need to be discarded. They are the perpetuation of what someone else believes strongly which work or worked for them. We can respectfully let go as we move toward embracing those values which carry us toward realizing the potential created in each of us by a Creator who seems to delight in our discovery of what has been hidden away in this complex package of our being.

## *Summary*

The presence or absence of clear values will determine how successfully you live. Take some time to review the primary values you now live with. are they consistent with where you're going? Do they need to be modified or discarded? State clearly for yourself what you will choose to be the foundational values you operate with from here. Live out your values with determination. Discard the inhibiting ones with courage. Embrace the new ones with hope. Don't turn back.

# 10

## *Feeling And Focus*

Feelings are the blessing and curse of human experience. They provide the coloration and enrichment of what we believe and experience. They add dimension, size, shape and enrich the boredom of facts, figures and skeletons. At the same time, feelings introduce a maze of confusion and internal experiences which pit truth against perceptions, reality and potential against fear and hope, and demonstrate the capability to turn optimism and motivation into apathy.

One of the common responses most people have to feelings is an assumption which goes something like: "If I feel it, it must be true." If your feeling response to a situation is let's say anxiety, that feeling is generally telling you that you are unable to handle the situation, and that the outcome is not going to be pretty. One of the skills that will help us live more successfully, is to make decisions about feelings rather than run with whatever we feel.

Any number of factors contribute to how we feel about an experience. In short, we can be preconditioned by experiences to produce a particular feeling response. It can be a singular event, or a series of events which create this conditioning. Ironically, it just seems to be the negative ones which we allow to control our perceptions, not the positive ones.

A number of years ago an older gentleman was referred to me by his physician. He was a man in his seventies who had been attacked by a dog while he was out on a walk. This formerly vibrant, active and virile man was now withdrawn, afraid and impotent. He was experiencing a major fear reaction every time he saw any kind of dog. It didn't matter if the dog was in a car, on a leash, tied up, or in a kennel. He had lost his ability to feel relaxed around dogs as he had all of his life.

His understandable feelings of fear had become superimposed on his old perceptions about dogs. These feelings were so profound, their message was telling him that any dog, under any circumstance, at any time, represented a major, life-threatening risk to him. His feelings were absolutely controlling him. The unfortunate aspect of his phobia, beyond the actual difficulty of the canine assault, was that the fear had become indiscriminate. It affected him in areas having nothing to do with dogs. He lost his confidence in small things: getting his car serviced, working on projects around the house, managing the most simple tasks. The fact of sexual impotence startled him further. To him this became a sign of the *truth* about his age, declining health, vibrancy, manhood, and the loss of the kind of life he enjoyed.

His response to a terrifying experience was a total redefinition of not only his belief about dogs and his level of risk about them, but his beliefs about general risks in life.

The moment of crisis or "psychological surprise" seems to present us with new definitions of our experience. It throws a new belief at us with convincing authority. The man who was attacked by a dog was so unsettled by the violence of the attack that he became convinced by his helplessness in that specific event that he was incompetent, stupid, mindless and easily overcome. How could he argue with these thoughts, particularly in view of the fact of his recent failure to adequately manage a serious event?

What is interesting is that the outside observer could just as easily draw entirely different conclusions about the meaning of the event that defined personal failure for the man. This particular dog was especially vicious and would frighten even the most fearless, dog-loving soul. It certainly would have rattled my cage. There was nothing cowardly about retreating from this dog, or being unsettled about the attack.

But to this mild, gentle man, the psychological surprise of the attack was something entirely outside of his experience. In that moment of shock he was overwhelmed and confronted with a new consideration: "If what he believed about dogs wasn't true, maybe what he believed about himself wasn't true." In his mind, the attack assumed the dimension of treachery on the same level as if he had suddenly discovered that his retirement fund had been embezzled by a trusted manager.

It is not uncommon for any of us who choose to live outside of a protective cocoon and reach for a certain quality of life, to get blindsided by something we just didn't see coming. That surprise is accompanied by the inability to define or categorize the experience, which is even more disturbing. It is difficult to get going again without a sense of caution, until we find some way to define or label the experience, and put it to rest. In psychological jargon, we call that closure.

In 1981 I flew over the remains of what used to be the beautiful and symmetrical Mount St. Helens in Washington State. I had circled, crossed and flown by this inspiring mountain dozens and dozens of times. I knew its shape, size, location, and features almost as well as the topography of my own middle-aged face. My first flight over the mountain, a couple of months after the catastrophic eruption, left me in a state of wordless shock. There was no frame of reference in my mind for what I saw. It simply wouldn't fit anywhere. I had never seen anything that even remotely resembled the view from my plane.

Perhaps the best way to describe it was that it looked like a scene from a science fiction movie filmed on an "other world" location. This colorless grey expanse of destroyed earth, trees and water were rearranged, disordered and a scattered mess. It was the romper room aftermath of a cosmic teenage no-holds-barred party of epic proportions.

The picture just didn't fit. I circled the mountain several times, trying to get the picture to register; it never did. The photographs I took only bring back the memory, but there is still no place for it. Life does bring those catastrophic surprises. Mountains explode, dogs attack, bank accounts are pilfered, lovers leave, friends die, the predictable ceases, the unknown becomes our experience.

The fact that surprises are there is positive. If things can change that radically, in such epic proportions, why not good and unimaginable change as well? We can be surprised into wonderful change, accomplishment and recovery. We just have to move in the right direction and listen to the right voices. The critical thing about feelings is that they are the least representative source of measuring truth and possibilities. Tragically, to one extreme some people have been so overwhelmed by feelings, that they have learned to cut themselves off from them, and now live a colorless life. The better option is to recognize them as often poor representatives of what is really happening, particularly when we're being "stretched." We cannot afford to discard the ability to feel. However the ability to manage our lives well includes the skill of managing feelings of fear, and learning not to trust our perceptions when fear has us by the ears.

It is interesting that in athletics even conditioned athletes "stretch" before a competition or a significant exertion. If the muscles could talk (actually they do through pain sensations), they would say, "Hey, what are you doing stretching me like that; that hurts. It is a major discomfort. It is clear that you shouldn't do that. This activity is certainly not good for you." Translated, this comes through like: "If it feels uncomfortable, you shouldn't do it." One perception could be, "If you are going to run a race, you should rest for several days in advance." Reality, on the other hand, indicates another perception is necessary.

As we deliberately label and define an experience like this, we do not have to decide what it means every time it occurs. That perception then gives us the freedom to keep moving, albeit sometimes at an altered pace, toward what we want.

The voice of reason, sometimes shouted down by our well-endowed lungs of protest, says: "Listen; we're just going through the preparatory stages of readiness to accomplish something fantastic." It further states, "Pain and discomfort are absolutely wonderful. It is waking up your system to enjoy the surprise of a new level of performance and accomplishment that you can't even imagine."

A patient who is in recovery from a traumatic injury has no frame of reference with which to understand the process of pain, discomfort, and the value of the tedious steps of physical therapy. Logic and feelings come to a rare point of agreement here. It is inconceivable that recovery and healing are accomplished through purposefully creating more discomfort. There is no psychological readiness or understanding of the sense of it. Everything inside resists the idea that the pain and grind of physical therapy, rather than rest and relaxation, facilitate healing and the restoration of abilities lost.

Feeling good is necessarily preceded by feeling bad; sometimes real bad. My favorite *Star Trek* character, Dr. Spock, the ultimate cognitive creature, would have no difficulty with this concept. But most of us have one heck of a time accepting the idea. If we had our way, life would be painless — and dull. We need the color and richness which being creatures of feelings allows us. We also need to know when to listen, when to question, and when to absolutely overrule feelings.

I recently saw an interview on television with Mark Martin, a NASCAR racecar driver. He was being interviewed on the heels of a very successful season. His comments were delightfully insightful in his down-home, southern good-old-boy wisdom. He talked with the interviewer about "the year of good and bad." He said it well with: "We learned a few things from the good — and a lot from the bad." That was his perceptual decision, to choose to label events in a way that allowed him to appreciate all of what happened, take away the potential for getting worried about more of the same, and then move on with enthusiasm to his next season.

Some people do so well with functional or "practical" intelligence that they never try to integrate it with formal intelligence. This is where "street smarts" tries to do without much factual information. "Savvy" without information can get a person a long way toward some goals, but eventually leads to closed doors. Good formal intelligence, on the other hand, if not coupled with some functional "savvy," can leave bright people with the frustration of not getting the job done because of, well, stupid mistakes. One of the aims of this book is to introduce the idea of functional intelligence as an asset to the management of feelings. This is a core issue for those who have the ability to accomplish great and small things, but never seem to completely get there. It is also an issue for those of great brilliance whose personal lives just don't reach an adequate level of fulfillment. It is an issue for the CEO, the successful entrepreneur, the accomplished professional, and the brilliant business executive.

As amazing as it sounds, many people just do not know what they are feeling. When this is the case, the presence of those feelings has a great impact on a person's level of effectiveness at what he is trying to accomplish. The nearby observer will readily see him engaged in anger, fear, love or infatuation and notice the shock or surprise of the person acting out should his feelings become identified to him. This does not imply denial, just lack of awareness.

Recently, my teen-age daughter and a group of girl friends were doing their "girl thing." One of her long-standing friends has some peculiar traits which my daughter has observed as part of her friend's personality for years. During this particular time together, this girl's quirks were mentioned in their bantering with each other. At first embarrassed and afraid of her identified differences, something great happened. She had carried a feeling for years that if these things were known, she would be ridiculed out of the group she wanted to belong to. She had spent a great deal of energy trying to hide what had been obvious to her friends for years. Gladly what she discovered was that it didn't really matter. In this case, fear of discovery resulted in the warmth of acceptance.

The sad part of course, is that she had lived with an unnecessary perception of herself that kept her in hiding, afraid of discovery, and having negative feelings about herself. The myth she believed was that it was not her real self which was cared for, but rather the projected, and less-than-complete self that was accepted.

It is one thing to feel something. It is another thing to know how we feel about what we feel.

An occasional occurrence in the therapy setting is the emergence of personal feelings a client begins to have for his therapist. For example, as a male therapist with a female client, as I listen, understand, support, encourage and develop a level of connection with a client, I can become the idealized spouse, father, lover, friend, or—a process called transference. The feelings the client may have may reflect those she might feel toward someone with whom she was in a close relationship. Not understanding that process of feelings and responding to them in kind becomes "expensive" if not dealt with professionally.

Conversely, for the therapist whose client hangs on every word, and who is appreciative of the knowledge and expertise demonstrated by the therapist, the respect given is welcomed. The feelings on the part of the therapist, normal responses to appreciation and respect are healthy in the appropriate context. But to transfer the glow of approval to the client is inappropriate, because to do so redefines the professional relationship into a personal one. That side of the coin is called countertransference. The purpose and effectiveness of therapy is destroyed.

We all have strong and intense feelings about situations and people. That in itself is nothing more than a fact of having feelings generated in different situations. What we do to manage those feelings is a demonstration of the presence or lack of emotional maturity.

Emotional maturity is defined as the ability to do things gracefully and efficiently. How does one do that? You start with an honest awareness of how you feel. Then, you go on to learn how to manage, not deny, those feelings. For example, to be afraid and stressed in a new business venture is not a betrayal of the entrepreneurial spirit. To feel anxiety, in the pursuit of a dream is not unusual. Lack of motivation to pursue your dream on a particular day may only mean that you have run your creative batteries down and need to get them recharged. To feel discouraged about the rate of progress in physical recovery is a positive sign — it means only that you are clear on where you want to be, but aren't there yet. The message is not, "Buck up, get moving, and quit feeling sorry for yourself." Rather it is a deliberate perception of the process based in reality, "This is part of what a motivated person deals with — the frustration of reaching for a goal." We need to be positive agents to help focus these pictures so that someone can define his situation in a way that allows him the perceptions to keep moving.

We cannot afford to nourish the myth of perpetual motion, unlimited energy and boundless enthusiasm. All of those wonderful experiences come from a reservoir which needs to be continually fed and replenished. Feelings of fatigue, of being out of focus, or just plain grumpy, may only be the internal energy banker sending you an overdraft notice. All of us need to build emotional bank accounts from which we can draw fresh perspectives. I call this "Emotional Fiscal Management," or simply "Emotional Banking." Like normal banking, the emotional account requires adequate deposits to cover withdrawals—emotional upheavals, and the demands of day-to-day expenditures on whatever we're dealing with.

The emotional bank account represents the ability all of us possess to ebb and flow, stretch and contract, and experience the range of feelings between stress and relaxation. If you notice your colleagues giving you that, "What's your problem today?" look, it is probably a good sign for you to make some deposits in your emotional bank account.

A nap, a quick trip to a refreshing place, or some other band-aid for intervention, is a priority. That is an important perceptual overlay — a temporary reprioritization. All of the things demanding your attention are still as important as ever, however, the ability to manage them effectively decreases dramatically if we do not rebuild the resources we need to make good judgments and choices about what to do. "I can't afford to take the time right now" is a high-risk perception. Without the emotional and physical resources, we often manage things so that they take more effort later on to clean up and fix. While the emotional account is in trouble, don't expect yourself to judge what you feel, see, think or perceive with any degree of accuracy. To stop the intake of data through a distorted filter is the first step in plugging the drain hole in your emotional bank account. Simply put, stop listening to the confused messages floating around in your head. To do that sometimes requires getting focused or involved in something else for a while that captures and holds your attention elsewhere. The next step is for you to make some substantial deposits in your account to enable you to sustain normal emotional daily withdrawals. What that is will of course vary for each of us — the point is, find *something*.

I had a middle-age male client who had held about fifteen jobs in the twelve months before we met. He was bright, talented, likable, and miserable. He had left each job because it didn't live up to the potential he believed it represented. His family was going to pieces, his wife was distraught due to the stress of constant change and financial instability. The energy, drive, enthusiasm, and hope he invested in each job gave him no return and depleted his mental and emotional energy. By the time I saw him, he was spent.

The unknown goal he pursued was the perfect job. To him, he was a good provider, spouse, father, businessman only if he absolutely maximized every moment and opportunity which presented itself. When his jobs did not match his overblown expectations, he quit and looked for another opportunity that would match his unrealistic dreams. His emotional bank account was drained as a result of one disappointment after another. The sad truth is that there were in reality no significant disappointments in any of his ventures, except when measured against a perfectionistic standard. Any one of the jobs he had did, in fact, have realistic potential to provide a good and stable income.

Everybody is vulnerable to some form of unreal expectation. It can be money, prestige, sex, material things, power and who knows what else. If we allow ourselves to become convinced that we must do our absolute maximum best at everything, that pertains to our expectations, then we put ourselves at risk. It is far better to lean way over in the direction of balance in our lives. This requires self-care, doing things that give us energy, joy and enthusiasm in order to give them back to other people, things and activities.

One of the interesting current trends among the middle-aged set, has to do with Harleys. Yes, those noisy, two-wheeled, chrome and "bad" bikes. No longer the venue of just bad boys, the professional and business set has rediscovered a piece of American lore to be enjoyed underneath their Levis. A recent report on this phenomenon indicated that these were the new toys for successful men and women "who have deprived themselves" while building careers. I thought that was an interesting perspective. If that assessment is true, it is too bad. We all need things that feed us at some level — make all that we do worth it. The challenge is to have that going on all of the time, to keep the emotional account balanced. Otherwise we may adopt a sad "wait-for-retirement" posture instead of living a full life.

We must identify the resources outside of ourselves to draw from for strength, enthusiasm and courage. It takes investigation and trial and error to find those ideas, activities and people which help to keep us inspired and energized.

The place where most of our feelings come from is a reservoir of perceptions and beliefs. It is important that when we talk about managing feelings, or emotional maturity, that we understand what we can do to contribute to a good perceptual framework.

It always amazes me that so few people understand that if we are going to have healthy feelings and perceptions, we must build a foundation for them. Having a life that is in focus, balanced and successful in accomplishing what we want to do, goes well beyond just managing emotions. First, we must eliminate toxic influences.

A Biblical gem of insight says, "A man is known by the kinds of friends he chooses," and makes the obvious point that like-minded people wind up together. It also implies the important understanding that we have significant influence on and gain experience from those we are around. There have been a couple of memorable times in my life when it became crystal clear that I had to make some choices about some of my friendships.

A number of years ago I met a couple who were a lot of fun to be around. They both had a great sense of humor, enjoyed a variety of activities, and were always up to do something fun or exciting. They were good friends, were always ready to be helpful, and were there if needed. What took some time to discover was how toxic they really were.

I began to wonder why I felt so strange after being with them for some time. On the surface things were pleasant. At first, I thought that I was just being strange. As I began to pay attention to what was really going on, however, I made an unsettling discovery: they loved dirt. Not the kind dealt with by shovel or vacuum cleaner. "Dirt" as in what so-and-so did to so-and-so, who made what recent mistake, who was ready to get done in by whom, and what inside stories were known about whom. Their fun personalities became polluted by their accounts of misery, misfortune and gossip about other people. I remember going home at times feeling like I needed a bath; the focus had become toxic.

I found myself becoming critical, sarcastic, and entertained by the conversations that these friends were so good at sharing with great humor and fun. If we are trying to function at a level of emotional maturity, it cannot be done beyond the scope of the environment we create for ourselves. I was inadvertently creating a perceptual environment that looked for what was wrong, who messed up, what happened to whom, etc. It is not possible to live in that kind of a world of experience and conversation, and at the same time learn to be mature in managing our own emotions. Our emotions are directly managed by the perceptions of the world we choose to live in on a daily basis.

Eventually I withdrew from the friendship with this couple. It was really too bad, because the truth is they were a lot of fun. The other side of the coin however, was that the relationship was very expensive. The couple represented values antithetical to where I wanted to go. At the risk of this sounding judgmental and stuffy, the reality is that we are influenced by what we regularly expose ourselves to, including the attitudes and perceptions of the world around us.

Being emotionally mature has demands, the first of which is recognizing that we cannot afford the luxury of anything, anyone, or any perception that is toxic. They are emotional carcinogenics that destroy our ability to function maturely. It is not possible to be graceful, efficient, critical, pessimistic, idealistic or perfectionistic all at the same time.

The point is not to try to isolate ourselves from anything or anyone who is the least bit toxic. Our emotional immune systems can handle a fair amount of that. There is a point at which that immune system does become incapable of maintaining health. It is our responsibility to manage our intake accordingly to maintain our emotional maturity.

I watched a business colleague struggle with this. He was a

competent professional in his field. He was a visionary, capable of blending the entrepreneurial spirit with appropriate caution and wisdom. He had on his own developed a very successful business. He then faced a reality common to many: grow or maintain a low profile. He chose to grow.

He did a good job of developing a plan to facilitate the growth he wanted to achieve in his business. He created a workable structure to bring in production and support staff to get things rolling. He interviewed and hired the people to get the job done. He hired well-trained capable people to work for the firm. He did almost everything right.

He made one critical mistake. He assumed that all of the people brought in to do this job were: as serious as he was about getting the job done, and all willing to work together with a good attitude to solve whatever problems came up to get to the goals at hand. Major mistake in assumptions!

As the initial honeymoon of this venture wore off some problems surfaced. It became clear to him that a couple of the staff had a proverbial "axe to grind." Two of the female staff carried around a strong feminist agenda. They had a predisposition to expect unfair, gender-biased actions to be a part of any company policy or decision-making. All staff meetings, planning meetings and attempts at decision-making became terribly bogged down with this unresolvable perceptual bias.

For what it is worth, this guy is probably one of the most fair, pro-people, pro-women, pro-independent-thinking people I know. He was fair to a fault, and himself got bogged down in the internal toxic chaos that began to breed. In talking with him during this process, he had a hard time making some difficult choices. He felt that he had assembled a good team (which he had), that the business needed the expertise that each of these individuals represented (and it did), and therefore he couldn't afford to make any significant changes in his personnel if he wanted to get the job done (major mistake).

Eventually the internal chaos of this potentially successful company brought progress to a screeching halt. The combination of his initially faulty perceptions of the people he hired, and the inability to see the toxic influences that some of the people brought with them made a promising business a place whose full time occupation became conflict management.

Even though he could well be described as a functionally and emotionally mature person, the environment he participated in took on a life of its own beyond his ability to manage it. The only eventual solution was to dismantle part of the team and start over, having learned some painful lessons. At least that was a posture of emotional maturity — to recognize the toxic situation, to dismantle it, and to create a healthier foundation to build an effective organization..

He did reorganize, redirect his energy, and become part of a team that got the job done. The original problem wasn't managed as efficiently as it could have been because of his perceptual framework, simply a failure to recognize the power of an internal toxic influence and deal with it accordingly. The perception of needing each staff person who had been assembled as a key ingredient to success allowed the situation to develop as it did.

A more effective perception was that each *role* that had been identified and staffed was indeed important. More importance had been given to the employees technical skill level than an ability to work together with a good problem-solving attitude. Obviously we're not looking at trying to create a perfect environment, rather a willingness to give attention to very real factors beyond technical expertise in the development of greater effectiveness.

This is not a cavalier attitude that expects people to always agree, go with the program or be gone. It is rather a willingness to take a new look at things when they are not working.

Recently I saw an interview on television with the actor James Earl Jones. Besides his great voice and talent as an actor, he expressed a gem of wisdom. In a recent movie release he plays the part of a black minister in the South during the forties, who preceded and inspired Dr. Martin Luther King and the entire Civil Rights Movement. He was reflecting on the unfortunate lack of completion of the inspiration that drove this important movement in our country. It has nothing to do with an inadequacy of the moral mandate, but rather the loss of what he called, "the second fire." His observation was astute to say, "the second fire is the bootstrap effect." He explained that to be taking personal responsibility, self enterprise to keep the flame alive.

If our feelings of disappointment or frustration are processed with the perception that someone else, something else, should be taking care of our problem, we are only left to protest. Protest is an important first step, but bootstraps are" the second fire," the only guarantee of the completion of anything that is significant. Athletes talk a lot about the "second effort," the push-back at resistance. If we are going to manage feelings well, we must operate with the perception that there will be obstacles — sometimes significant and relentless ones. There will be any number of things beyond our control or making that will raise their ugly heads. The "second fire" is the perception that refuses to be naive, and accepts the need to take personal responsibility for whatever we must do. Without that perceptual resolve, we cannot manage feelings or consequences, and therefore will never live with any degree of emotional maturity, or as we have also called it — functional intelligence.

Once we have become clear on this, we need a means of maintaining that focus. This goes back to something we have discussed before. It is here that we can use those perceptions we have deliberately decided ahead of time to embrace and use to process events as well as feelings.

If we are conditioned to have, let's say, a fear response to a situation, we need to use the decisiveness of a different perceptual tool as an alternative to feeling fear. For example, a person who has gone through the pain and chaos of a divorce is likely to have reason to respond in fear to having a new spouse become upset or express frustration with their relationship. I heard a tape on which Tony Robbins, one of the gurus of self empowerment, used a wonderful perceptual tool to manage the old feeling responses: "The past does not equal the future." I might add, "unless you start to respond to the present problems in the same way." Taking that perception, which may not be felt, or even believed, but used to deliberately look at whatever is going on, is a powerful tool.

It absolutely does not matter that you may not feel in a way consistent with that perception. It simply becomes the lens through which you CHOOSE to look to manage a particular feeling that otherwise is destructive. It is the means of maintaining a focus and direction, rather than getting distracted or overwhelmed by feelings that control you. The focus is more important than the picture.

I want to be careful at this point to reiterate an important piece of information. Not all feelings are the result of perceptions and beliefs. Our bodies being the bio-electro-chemical systems they are, do produce the stimuli for feelings of depression, anxiety, paranoia, and others beyond the scope of what we create from perceptions. When an endogenous based depression exists, (as distinguished from exogenous — created by external events), one produced by this bio-chemical process, one cannot manage it just with perceptual changes. However, the intensity of it can certainly be influenced by one's perception of the events at the time. In this case medical intervention is critical as an important foundation to treatment. The tools that we're discussing here can be of wonderful secondary help in learning how to look at the whole process in a way that enhances one's recovery.

The management of feelings also has a positive side that can be of significant help in managing forward-moving direction. There are for all of us those moments of inspiration and excitement about things. Sometimes it is the fun we're having with friends, or perhaps the excitement of participating in an activity that "gets the old juices flowing." It is also that feeling of clear-focused excitement when we are able to capture a vision about the possibilities in something. It is this last process to which I want to give particular attention.

This book is intended to be a guide to help people get where they want to go. It is a source book for dreamers, those who want to get past the present limitations or circumstances of their lives. For this process to occur, there must be a starting point. There has to be a point of inspiration, or vision to act as a catalyst to the process of change.

You have heard people refer to projects, businesses, teams and people as "uninspired." Basically this assessment means, boring, without spark or life. The kind of process I want to help facilitate is more complete LIVING. Obviously, that implies something that is alive, has energy and is moving. That cannot exist, much less reach a point of completion, without starting out with inspiration.

There are two important sides to managing feelings; the first is to manage the negative ones which will flatten any creative process, the second is to learn how to keep alive the positive feelings of inspiration and vision. It is important to be able to experience, capture, and keep alive those positive feelings that strike us. They are of phenomenal importance, and must be highly valued and protected if we are to realize the things we want to experience. We cannot live in a state of epiphany, but can capture the essence of those moments of clear focus for a direction and momentum.

I think everyone knows what it is like to get really excited about something. We also know the (sometime later) experience of trying to remember what on earth we were so excited about. When we are filled with the charge of excitement, the vision of the potential for ourselves, there is a period of disregard for what might be involved in getting to the point of securing this job. Inspiration allows us to believe that what we want is there, it can be done, there are no unsurmountable obstacles, and we can see ourselves in the new position. There is that momentary emotional experience as if we were actually there, enjoying the fulfillment of the dream. Then something happens.

It is like the good news/bad news report from the car salesman. "I can get you the exact car you want, and you can drive it home today, but the payments will be somewhat higher than you wanted to pay, because I cannot give you as much trade-in value for your old car." Excitement shifts from visualizing yourself driving your new car home, to the basic issue we all face every day — price tags. It brings us back to assessing the worth to us.

I think this is why refrigerator magnets were invented. They are used to hold up pictures of slim bodies, fast cars, new furniture, boats or a vacation hideaway. They have become the tools of the shrine for dreams. They are the guideposts for this sacred ground. They hold up what people value the most.

The point is simple. It is important somehow to be able to capture things or images that keep alive the FEELINGS of those things, dreams, goals and people that are important to us. "Out of sight, out of mind" is a reflection of the truth that even deeply-felt feelings need to be nurtured to be kept alive.

When you get touched with a positive feeling, vision, or focus of inspiration, capture it because you will need to be deliberate in keeping it alive. The feelings we choose to nurture and feed, do drive us. The absence of positive feelings on the other hand is a paralytic force.

## *Summary*

Once you are clear on the focus you want to maintain toward whatever goals you are establishing, find or create a symbol to help keep both the focus and the feelings about that outcome alive. It may be a picture, a saying, or a physical object. It can be anything you can display conspicuously in a place you will see it often. The idea is to remind you of where you are going and keep positive feelings alive about your objective.

# 11

## *Intimacy, Problem Solving, And Other Crises*

⬅――――――――
　　―――――――――➡

It seems to me from the vantage point of therapist, consultant and life observer, that we are at regular odds with how things are in contrast with how we want them to be. Let's take intimacy for example. It often feels fool-hardy to approach this subject about which so much is stated, written, and argued, and at the same time, apparently understood so little.

My definition of intimacy is simple: Safety. A state requiring no guard, threat, or self protection. A state in which, because of the lack of guard, it is possible to bond and "connect" with someone in a way that is mutually satisfying and beneficial. Many things enhance that state; many things also jeopardize it. Only one thing maintains it. Like all of the issues being approached in this book, how we see, interpret and perceive those things, makes all the difference. This is, if possible, even more so the case of this often pursued, and equally as often lost, sense and experience of intimacy, closeness of connection with someone or something of importance.

It is ironic, that the issues which enhance intimacy, and those which jeopardize it, are the same: problems. Problems carry with them the potential to disconnect. They can disconnect us from people, goals, things, dreams, anything of value. The loss of any of these valued assets can be as poignant as the loss of an intimate relationship.

We all experience loss differently. Some vow never to get so involved again, others rebound right into another replacement. To lose intimacy is a loss of safety, and ultimately, the ability to function spontaneously at our best. Many people perceive this event as an indication that the sense of intimacy is no longer possible in their particular situation, therefore it must be found somewhere else. However, that becomes a treadmill that gives nothing but short term relief from the intimacy crisis. To regain it requires risk-taking with a different view. The deliberate view is that problem-solving, not replacement, is a legitimate tool to *maintain* intimacy. In other words, it is not a state that either does or does not exist. It is rather one that has the inherent ebbs and flows of circumstances that provide the stage on which to work the process of *intimacy*. Therefore, we must embrace the perception that problems are absolutely necessary — the catalysts to develop the skills to maintain that sense of safety. We can learn to choose a perception, a label placed on those events, to see them as necessary agents to maintain intimacy, rather than expend our energy to avoid, deny or protest. In this sense, one of the "best" experiences of my life was an inflight engine failure in my airplane several years ago.

Every pilot who takes the job of flight management seriously wonders what he would really do when face to face with the emergencies he trains for. To be a pilot, or to do any thing which carries risk, involves either denial of risk, the willingness to manage risk or the arrogance of "I can do anything." Emergency flight training was born out of the recognition through experience of the potential problems encountered in flight. Problems are the necessary precondition to expertise and competence. Competence and success are not measured in the ability to beat the system, avoid pitfalls, or circumnavigate all potential negative experiences, but rather a willingness to manage the reality and experience any of those arenas present.

For a number of years, I had a satellite office for my practice out

### Intimacy, Problem-Solving, And Other Crises 161

of state. I commuted with my twin engine airplane each week, all year long. One December I was returning on my regular schedule back home under normal flight conditions for that time of year — multiple layers of clouds, snow and occasional light icing in the clouds. The first half of the one hour flight was uneventful. I climbed through the first layers of clouds, and was actually on top of it all in bright sun shine at 13,000 feet. It's hard to describe the exhilaration of flying in intensely clear blue skies on top of the beautiful but unpleasant whiteness below. That is one of the many experiences allowed to pilots which keep stimulating this curious passion for flying.

After a pleasant half hour in the winter sun at altitude, I was given step-down clearances to prepare for an instrument approach and home. "November 142 Foxtrot, you are cleared to descend on your present heading to 9,000 feet — then 5,000 feet." Suddenly, while in dense clouds descending at over 250 miles per hour, a whole new series of events were thrown at me and my faithful airplane. The airplane shuddered with an intense vibration, different noise patterns and an immediate dilution of my normal sense of comfort, safety and predictable flight experience.

What happened, was that the governor which manages the propeller speed failed, and immediately put the right engine propeller in flat pitch — kind of like shifting your car into first gear doing 90 miles per hour. Consequently the engine over-reved, I saw the tachometer for that engine swing past the red line, and then things started coming apart. There were literally engine parts going everywhere — what we call catastrophic failure — in other words, an expensive mess!

Success at managing anything, from an inflight crisis, to corporate profits to intimacy in relationships, can only be declared on the other side of a crisis, or failure. My inflight engine failure taught me many things. It confirmed others. What I hoped would be true proved itself as such—I am a good pilot, my training and experience set the stage not only to survive, but to experience the after-the-fact knowledge and satisfaction that the worst-case scenarios can be managed. One tends to approach future flights differently.

The experience of engine failure can either breed additional fear of realities, press toward more skill development, or arrogance and complacency. It is up to us to decide on the definition and perception we will maintain. That again depends on the outcome we want to achieve. One of the things I learned while managing my emergency was that although my skills in many areas were excellent, in some they were only adequate. Flying a multi-engine airplane on one engine is not all that difficult once you are trained and practiced. Add to that however, instrument conditions (flying in solid cloud conditions), some icing, minimums (low ceilings and visibility) at the destination, and things get very interesting and busy. All skills in flight management get put to the test, and weak links show up. I found a couple of them. Now come the perceptions and choices: Retreat and worry, deny and press on, or acknowledge and fix.

The most common responses to crisis I see are the first two. Unfortunately, if we don't have the failure experience followed by the opportunity to develop additional skills for the next time (there will be one), we are left feeling that there are no reasonable options other than worry or bravado. Intimacy acknowledges reality. Safety — my definition of intimacy — is not jeopardized by challenges or threats to it. Safety is evolutionary, and must be, because circumstances are as well. Therefore the form, structure, and tools of maintaining safety will occasionally change in response to the circumstantial changes around us. If we rigidly define safety, make it a fixed state, we destroy the foundation of our sense of willingness to invest in anything perceived or desired to be intimate.

It is important to understand that safety is not an accident. Nor is safety the absence of risk or trauma. It is rather the preparedness to deal with the realities that present themselves, or at least the willingness to deal with them. That is the only reason we can conscientiously remarry, start in business again, or do anything we believe we failed at before. Remember that the crisis event is not the measurement of the success or failure question; it is rather the juncture from which we determine success or failure, the point of choosing to manage what has happened to us and direct it toward a desired outcome.

Safety is created by a willingness to accept the realities involved, and an attitude to learn the skills to manage anything, and a perception that this is all a tribute to the person who will be whole and truly alive.

The tools required to manage the potential emergencies in the first, simple little two-place airplane in which I learned to fly were equally simple. If the single engine quits, its time to land; there are no other options. There is no landing gear to put down, no other engine to manage, no instrument approach available — the airplane doesn't have the instruments for that kind of flying. There is no high speed landing off an airport; this thing will land in a few hundred feet of almost anything from a road to a field to a good sized parking lot, at under 50 miles-per-hour.

Intimacy is easy in an environment which causes no distress. But that is like a statement made by the Christian statesman/author, Watchman Nee. In his book, *True Christianity,* he states that "true spirituality is always expressed in community." In other words, anyone can be spiritual all by himself. A monk on a mountain, an ascetic in isolation may enjoy the richness of spiritual fellowship with God. Does it count? Certainly in one restricted sense it does, but it is so limited.

True intimacy, like spirituality, absolutely must demonstrate its vitality and worth in unisolated environments and in response to everything that challenges and tears at it. Intimacy can possess no value and worth to us—is not worth the hope that it inspires—unless it can be born from and responds to the condition of our lives, problems, disappointments and loss.

Let me give you two examples on different sides of this issue. First, how not to do it.

I have had the opportunity to observe one particular team of professionals trying to build a successful health-care organization. At the core of the organization was an individual who was bright, capable and articulate. At a cognitive level, he had a thorough understanding of people, how they need to be treated in a business in order to be happy and productive. On a day-to-day functional level, however, he was absolutely toxic in his management of the business. Ultimately it failed because of him. Here's is how it went.

He had the ability to identify and solicit capable people into the business. He sounded good to the informed professional. However, once the team was assembled, little things began to change — always subtle and confusing. For example, these motivated and competent professionals were confronted with comments and questions from this person like: "Why did you say such and such to so and so when you contacted them," or "Did you know that so and so has been waiting for two minutes to see you," and any number of other "helpful suggestions."

The point is that the words that were used were not necessarily so toxic, as was the attitude and the condescending posture. In a very short time, the rhetoric of respect, camaraderie, and professional support were replaced with mistrust, suspicion and eventual withdrawal. Attempts by these colleagues to maintain "intimacy," or a functional environment by addressing the problem, were met with hostile/hurt denials. He would not be a player in problem-solving because his definition of intimacy was that he was doing everything right, and any discussion about problems was a confrontation of his integrity. The antithesis of intimacy was created out of its potential. In other words, the participants were all willing to be involved in a productive effort in the context that valued intimacy — a safe, mutually respecting environment. However, that enticing environment was used to seduce people into a position of control. Within a healthy organization or relationship, there is room for disagreement and differences, but not for a hierarchy which eventually prevents intimacy as I'm describing it.

The other side of intimacy is illustrated well by a person for whom I have a great deal of respect. I don't necessarily agree with him on everything, but his integrity demands respect. The name Billy Graham, will be known for centuries, as are other champions of faith and causes. In a time when any number of religious leaders, from money hungry Evangelists, to promiscuous preachers, to child molesting priests are capturing unwelcomed headlines, Billy Graham, as an acknowledged less-than-perfect human, demonstrates the integrity that is a part of any form of intimacy.

I believe that at the foundation of what he has demonstrated with what I call intimacy, is a foundation of honesty. Some time ago I saw a Barbara Walters interview him and his wife, Ruth. He made an interesting point that has been lost by many others. When he began his public ministry, several decades ago, he and his colleagues had some frank discussions about potential compromises to the intimacy they wanted to maintain with their families, each other, and God. Beyond their commitment to preaching the Gospel, was an equally strong understanding that less than scrupulous honesty with oneself would destroy whatever was accomplished. The seduction of money and women became points of discussion. This is not just a point of protecting intimacy with one's wife, but rather the intimacy with oneself and one's values to protect the ability to be effective, productive and successful at the goal before each of them.

They developed together a system of mutual accountability. This system was not restraint, but rather a benevolent safety measure to protect them from the consequences of the inevitable problems and risks that arise in any venture. This system became the foundation for their ability to function.

The result was the "safety" in investing with each other to realize common goals. It was as well the security and confidence in being truly known, and knowing others in the reality of risks, with love and respect, fully aware of pure humanness they all wore. The results for those who cared for them was the created ability to support them, sometimes at the great expense of loneliness and separation. You cannot expect to be supported in your goals and dreams, unless you do your part in creating an environment in which it is "safe" for those around you to do so. This is the "price tag" issue. How much is it going to cost, and is it worth it? The process of intimacy, that is acknowledging and addressing problems, sets the stage for it to take place. Safety is the stage on which we are allowed to experience the wonderful reward of that bond with people. This must be the way that the unconditional love of God which I learned about in Sunday School is demonstrated — through those with whom we create a sense of safety and bonding. That does, however, require the risk of full disclosure, our feelings, weaknesses, temptations, fears, etc. Only in that context do we ever know that it is the *real* self that is being loved and care for, not just the *projected* self.

While the process of problem-solving is a necessary bedfellow of intimacy, however we apply the concept, it should not be construed as a necessarily constant state. Some of the jargon of the psychology language are terms like "closure" and "resolution." Basically we mean: "Its a done deal." No more review and analysis; no more contemplation and discussion.

In order to maintain our investment in anything we hold of value, there must be a sense of resolution to issues and problems that challenge us. I would not want to imply that we expect immediate and complete closure—it's a process. But we should be able to see things improving, and have some sense of ultimate closure, even if it is long-term. I suppose "movement" is the operative word. I remember my first experience with panic. I was in an eight foot dingy with my mother. (My second memory of panic was also on a fishing trip with my mother.) I was probably as old as the boat was long. We rented it somewhere on Puget Sound, rolled down a ramp (that part was exhilarating) and then floated about. It was the floating about part that gave me the problem. My perceptual system of the day indicated that movement was good; as long as she was rowing and making progress, we would stay afloat. To stop was to sink. (Come to think of it ... I still feel that way!) I can remember the immediate and pervasive rise to fear as we began to float freely. In my mind there was definitely some necessary assistance required to maintain our above-the-surface state of dry and warm existence.

Our general sense of safety is not unlike that. We must have some sense of movement toward resolution, AND the ability to do something about it. Had I been rowing, I would have taken care of it. My only option, yet still an option, was to "encourage" my hapless mother to keep rowing. I seriously doubt that she understood my throat-constricted pleading for movement toward the global issue of resolution as anything other than whining. Whining works! Well, at least for the short term. Most whiners however are eventually blessed with the absence of anyone who cares. "Here's a quarter, call someone who cares," is captured by a Country and Western lyricist who understood that. I'm sure that line was written for the confirmed whiners of the world.

Movement is however, a component, or perhaps more accurately, a measurement, of the process of closure and resolution. When working with clients seeking help to resolve any of the goals, we always have to deal with the "Square One" phenomena. That is the normal and frustrating, often discouraging, spastic process of forward-backward, up-and-down movement toward goal accomplishment, or the feeling of being back to "Square One" when what feels like forward progress stops. The maintenance of intimacy, direction or safety in any undertaking, is dependent upon understanding and accepting the typical process of changing outcomes, and how to measure progress. That certainly also includes room for those times when things seem stalled. Progress cannot be measured in those moments. If we will choose to perceive them as normal to the process, we will waste less energy in fighting or protesting what is simply not going to change for that moment.

Intimacy and safety are born of threats. They are sustained by the resolution of crises. We have the choice of living within the relative comfort of fear, trying to avoid risk and threats, versus enduring the painfully born knowledge that security, safety exists. It has been hard fought, won, and now known to be ours. To know that risks and challenges to intimacy can be resolved, is to settle into safety. To settle into safety is to come to the stage of creative thinking, contemplation and managing the situation. To know that no resolution is realistically going to happen, is to be encouraged to choose to change and redirect. To fear and resist change is to live with the familiar, but the incomplete. We can make most things happen, at least some of the time, but do we really want those things that we have to force or work so hard to contain? We're left with only the subconscious awareness and insecurity of always having to remain vigilant to keep things together and on track. It robs us of the security and peace of the settledness of reciprocal interest, care and investment, of what we participate in. The decision to continue to manage a difficult situation or end the process is a judgment call. As someone well said: "The ability to exercise good judgment is based on experience. Experience comes from exercising bad judgment!" Managing problems, whether we have created them or not, is necessary to protect intimacy and success, and to preserve the ability to direct the kind of life we choose to have.

## *Summary*

Make a commitment to a problem-solving posture as a value beyond protesting or proving. Make a choice to see any problem as *necessary* to define the direction toward whatever kind of life you are trying to create. Name one problem that is *necessary* right now.

# 12

## *The Unfamiliar Friend*

The subject of faith is central to the theme of this book. Faith, or the absence of it, influences the way we perceive things. One definition of faith suggests that it is "the substance of things hoped for, the evidence of things not yet seen" (Hebrews 1:1). Faith is a creative force, a facilitator of natural law, a confronter of the law of least resistance. Faith plays havoc with the structural processes of the trained thinker and creates amorphous roadblocks for those who cling to the Scientific Method to explain life without spiritual meaning. Issues of faith break all the rules. The sensory measurements on which we depend for a sense of stability simply do not apply. They contradict the idea of faith, which is a belief in something that cannot be proved.

Faith involves stepping outside of the normal framework of reference, patterns of experience, ways of looking at things and changing the expectation of outcomes. Faith entices us to acts as unnatural as bungie jumping from a bridge, to act in place of every instinct of self preservation. That is one circumstance in which I will likely never try to exercise faith. My instincts for survival are simply too well developed.

When it comes to invitations to stretch ourselves outside of the normal boundaries of our perceptions, beliefs and ways of responding, most of us shrink away and say "No." Part of the problem is that most people simply do not realize the presence of that internal phenomenon, and its ability to respond in a way that has great personal benefit.

It makes absolutely no sense to discuss faith, in religious or lifestyle terms without understanding the need for it in the first place. To understand the function of faith, you must start with hope, "Faith is the substance of things HOPED for." Hope can be translated to mean desire, dreams, aspirations, visions—anything that represents stretching beyond our present circumstances — visual imagining of something beyond the present. Stretching is important because we don't grow except by reaching beyond our grasp.

Stretching means putting satisfaction aside. I'm personally glad that the Wright brothers weren't satisfied with bicycles as transportation. Their hope of flight created a winged invention that changed the world. I'm glad that Jonas Salk invented a vaccine for polio rather than use his energy to teach victims of polio how to cope with their disease. Hope has given birth to the often tumultuous and difficult process which created enormous change in the world. Let's not forget that many of those discoveries were stimulated out of a need created by crisis.

The emphasis here is not on events demonstrating world-shaking faith, but is centered on the importance of faith to the development of functional and successful perceptions in our lives.

I am really not sure if our lack of demonstrated faith is because we repress our dreams, or because we are so encumbered with day-to-day things that we never take time to listen to the inner voice that tries to nudge us into life-giving realizations and experiences that wait patiently for us. It may not even matter. What is important is for us to realize is that our experiences have created an internal editor in each of us who evaluates and scrutinizes ideas, thoughts and dreams. This editor passes on the viability of these ideas and thoughts given the "reality" we live with and puts in place the constraints to their performance born out of what we presently believe possible.

The real value of the internal editor is to redefine the possible for us so that we may stretch the limits of our imagination and embrace faith as an integral part of our growth. Whether we approach faith in a traditional context of spiritual life, or apply it to goals born in the heart, we enter into a world of spectacular color and hope.

Some people seem to have a confused idea about the function of faith. To them, faith means submission to sources, powers, and events outside of their control, and an acceptance of the outcomes. In this context an individual who tries to make something happen violates the principles of the universe. Some eastern religions teach values that basically restrain people from "interfering" with the course of events. Those events are by design, and ought not to be tampered with by human intervention. Some cultures teach to not interfere with the process by saving someone's life — that would be meddling with divine purpose. Many conservative Christians border on this approach in their confusion about following "God's Will." I will not argue that there is Divine intention in the outcome of human events, but it is not, in my theology, a matter of perpetuation of the emotional, psychological and spiritual immaturity in people by a directive parent-God, who hinders growth and development by proscribing narrow limits for them. To be willing to look past present experience, is to provide for ourselves an opportunity to "see" other options beyond what is familiar.

It is a risk-taking gesture to say, "I know what I want to do in my life." It does not contain the often implied self-indulgent arrogance of the self appointed omniscient. This perception encourages individual discovery and demonstrates maturity. The prerequisite is not the absolute knowledge of the rightness of the approach — but the rightness of making a choice to risk the discovery of the dream, and the willingness to develop abilities to solve the problems that stand in the way. The pivotal point of success is the freedom to make choices as a follow-up response to what has been stimulated as a result of a leap of faith to stretch past conventional views and believed possibilities.

One of the sad commentaries about our American culture at this time, revolves around this theme. The alarming rise of serious crime, particularly by young people, is a symptom that something is terribly amiss. We have sadly moved to an ideology that minimizes the idea of personal responsibility. Criminal behavior is predicated on poor living circumstances, and the result of being cheated by the system. A growing culture of self-identified victims is looking to someone else to carry the burden of response and resolution.

I can deeply empathize with those in trouble. As a society we must be compassionate and responsive to the genuine needs around us. At the same time, we have become so confused about the lines of personal responsibility, and have idealized the concept of open-mindedness to an extreme. We have forgotten the common horse sense that keeps a culture responsive to need and in balance with a clear and unequivocal expectation of individual responsibility for the ultimate condition of one's own life.

Without a working understanding of faith as I am presenting it there is no reason to change this personal or cultural disease. There must be some viable option available that makes accepting personal responsibility worth the effort and ultimately make some practical sense.

The first step of faith is a willingness to become slightly uncomfortable. We don't know where this thing will lead us. Theologians and philosophers call this the "Faith Leap." Stepping outside of the norms of familiarity involves this step. The second step is having something else to respond to. The truth is that in the restrained vacuum of our own existence it is often difficult to visualize anything other than our familiar existence. Someone else often is the catalyst of change by throwing something into our arena, an idea or a vision of what other choice exists. We must be confronted by experience other than ours if there will be a reason to learn about the leap of faith. This is an essential ingredient, often overlooked by the well-intended reformers, of the social condition of many who seem caught in poverty.

The malignancies in our culture will never change for those involved in them until there is another picture in front of them, and a reason to take the risk of believing it can be theirs. The "American Dream" is not enough motivation to try for those who believe it is someone else's dream. To them it is only a cruel reminder of what they cannot and will not experience. I believe this is a good reason to live with rage and resentment. A lack of reasonable hope does that.

Faith and hope are mutually dependent on one another. So are resignation and complacency. The kind of faith I am encouraging learning to use, is the only igniting agent that will start and sustain the process of a quality of life that we can dare call successful.

Faith doesn't say: "I know the outcome." It says, "I REALLY DON'T KNOW." Exercising faith has nothing to do with being sure about something. It is the willingness to release something, a perspective or belief that we feel sure about, and experience the outcome of an entirely different perspective.

I wish I could give everyone that YAHOOOO feeling I experienced on the mountain when I skied the deep snow with new equipment that finally allowed me to do what I had dreamed of for years. I have had this love/hate relationship with Warren Miller's ski movies. Those pictures of skiing through untracked, waist deep powder snow would drive me nuts. I had the desire, the ability, but the wrong equipment. The three elements finally came together.

What I can do is challenge you to find the pieces for yourself. Start by listening to what your heart hopes for and don't settle for less. Look for the pictures that stimulate that desire, then keep feeding it. Take the leap of faith to do *something* to allow you to experience a piece of the picture.

Being unsure is what makes risks gestures of faith, the "substance of things hoped for." Bravado has nothing to do with faith. Nor does ultra-confidence. It is interesting what happens to those faith-taken experiences. They are (those things hoped for) no longer unknown and unfamiliar outcomes. As our hoped-for experiences translate to actual known and experienced events, or "the evidence of things not yet seen," they become a new and comfortable level of existence. In that sense, we could consider the exercising of faith as the literal creative force of bringing something new into our frame of reference and experience. It no longer remains a foreign and unfamiliar entity. It allows us to get acquainted with what we can consider normal and standard. This applies not only to what we experience for ourselves, but what we witness as well.

Many of our present experiences or accomplishments may well

have seemed unreachable or intimidating in the past. Now, however, they are commonplace and familiar, therefore often not recognized as the present evidence of past "hoped-fors."

The other day I saw a great interview on the Phil Donahue show. He had four guests who had become very successful in business. Among them were Dave Thomas of *Wendy's Restaurants,* and Nancy Fields of *Mrs. Field's Cookies.* Each of the guests had demonstrated a willingness to take those leaps of faith that were the key starting point to their phenomenal successes.

I was particularly impressed with the way Nancy Field illustrated the demonstration of the kind of faith we're discussing. She recalled an incident from a number of years ago which pushed her to do something with her life. She had married a successful economist, about 10 years her senior while she was still quite young. At a dinner party one evening hosted by a colleague of her husband's, during the course of conversation, she mispronounced a word. The less-than-gracious host, got up, took a dictionary from the shelf, and threw it on the table admonishing her with the words: "If you can't use the English language properly, you'll never amount to anything!"

Being totally humiliated, followed by a period of tears and shame, she made a resolution to do something significant with her life. Up to this point, she had been little more than an attractive trophy on her husband's arm. She had no clear sense of what to do.

After a period of brainstorming, she decided to take something she already loved and was good at, and make it into a business — cookies. Well, the response she received from literally everyone was not much different than most of us would give: "You're going to do what?" Everyone, including her husband, bet against her. Dear husband bet her that she wouldn't sell $50 worth on her first day. She sold $75. She had to leave her store-front to do it — no one came in. She hit the sidewalks with sheets of freshly baked cookies, and started acting toward the leap of faith of her new perception — that she could make a business out of her talent.

She had no empirical evidence to base that perception on. No one gave her the idea, much less supported her. She just did it. It is interesting to observe that she as a person was not on the line here — just the viability of cookies as a profit-making venture. If we tie self-esteem, our personal worth to a new venture or leap of faith, we will get nowhere. Who wants to take a chance to find out that one is worth nothing, that one is a failure? We must separate those issues. Likewise, we do not want to base self worth on a success, because if the venture fails our worth is the same as a failed venture.

If we want to hope and dream we must feed ourselves a diet to stretch beyond the normal and predictable. We must take those leaps of faith in our own experience, and we must watch for new experiences, outside of our present frame of reference, to provide us with the necessary evidence to continue.

We could call it the "Dream Diet." It would expose us to stimulants to bring other possibilities, other perceptions of ourselves, our situations, and all of the potentials to life. Beyond bringing something to life, is the nurturing of it, sustaining the now born potential to its maturity.

It is at this point that we can be very deliberate about exposing ourselves to the people and the stories of those who model the process of embracing new perceptions of things, and learning the tools to get from adjusting perceptions which allow the stretching we're discussing, to the realization of things once thought to be out of reach.

Faith helps us to exercise deliberate action which influences the outcomes we want in our lives. Sunday mornings will occasionally find me with Dr. Robert Schuller and *The Hour Of Power* telecast. Every time I have listened to him I have been inspired and focused in some special way. Beyond the ideas and perspective that make up the sermon for the day, I am always left with something else. I always feel settled, at peace, clear on what I want to do and I am motivated. Why? Something inside of us gets touched when we are fed a diet of hope, possibilities, and the reality of what faith can do. Faith rarely calls us to itself in a vacuum of our own perception of things. It requires exposure and stimulation from sources beyond the scope of our normal views and ideas.

If our perceptions are born from a focus on the obstacles we are experiencing, the problems to be solved and the unanswered questions we only perpetuate existing stagnation. If, on the other hand, something stimulates our "mental metabolism" to activation, that is the spawning ground for what is already in the heart. It just helps it to develop from germination to a fully living thing. When the perceptions we embrace are inspired by not only the truth of what is possible, but an ongoing diet of people, information, tools and gestures of faith which reinforce that dream, it will happen. All that remains is the time and tenacity it takes to get to that point of dream realization.

Look at the people you bring into your inner circle of influence. Look at the literature, the sources of thoughts and ideas you draw from. It is one thing to decide to learn how to exercise faith, it is another to be exposed to people, ideas and perspectives which do little but starve out and crush those ideas. I long ago learned that there are some people in my circle of acquaintances and friends that I don't share some things with, particularly my new, infant ideas. When ideas and dreams are new, they are extremely fragile, easily obliterated by someone who has different values.

If we want to grow and stretch in an area of life that is important to us, and we share those infant ideas with someone who's greatest value is comfort, security, and no risk, the idea coming to life can be be easily extinguished. This isn't because the other person is necessarily wrong or uninspired. He simply values something else for himself. That's fine. He's just the wrong person to consult at that stage. As we grow, we must realize that the people with whom we have always related well, will likely no longer be that same source of support and encouragement. Not because they've changed or abandoned their support of us, rather we have changed and abandoned a piece of commonly held and valued perceptual real estate. This is a no-fault dynamic, but one that is critical to understand.

Of the clients I have seen in my office over the years, many were victims of domestic violence and spousal abuse. One wonders why a bright, capable and good person would not only put up with abuse, but more often than not, return to the spouse only to be revictimized. Frequently when working with both men and women who have been a part of a chronically abusive relationship, it becomes clear that the patterns of the spouse are not going to change, and they must withdraw from the relationship if they are to survive.

For them to do so requires two leaps of faith. First, to redefine their existing faith, "They didn't mean to hurt me" or "They have promised to change, and I believe they will." must be viewed as no longer a viable focus of their hope. They often must also redefine existing "faith" which believes that they are not capable of having any kind of quality life on their own without the material benefit the abusive spouse provides.

Second, they must find a way to embrace a new focus of faith — not only can they survive a difficult transition, but even thrive because of it. Sadly, this doesn't happen as often as I would like to see. Part of the reason is the insidiousness with which new faith can be extinguished. The most effective deterrents to faith are criticism, attack and questioning. It is difficult to defend a new view. The same is true whether these toxic perceptions come from other people or from ourselves.

One couple I worked with demonstrated this with tragic clarity. As is often the case, she had been raised in an abusive family. He was pure military. Not a good combination! She was originally referred to me by her physician to treat her depression. He was happy to see her finally going "to get fixed." Within a very brief period of time, the source of her depression became clear. She could do nothing right, say nothing right, had no ability to understand anything of importance, and was lucky to have such a capable husband.

Initially I worked with her alone, and watched this timid woman start to come to life. She began to allow herself to take a leap of faith toward a realistic and healthy view of herself. Some wonderful changes began slowly to take place that left her happier and certainly more confident.

I began to include the husband in therapy as she started to stabilize. The hope is always to help facilitate some shifts in the interpersonal dynamics of the relationship to make it a healthier environment for both parties. Shortly my prognosis became something like, "Fat chance!" Occasionally when I listen to what people say, I wonder: "Do they have any idea what they are saying?" Clearly, he didn't. Comments to his wife like: "How can you be so dumb to believe that," or "Do you know what people *really* think about you?" or "You'll never change, it's a waste of my money for you to see this guy."

Not surprisingly, this couple eventually divorced. She continued to grow. What had become clear to her was that the faith she was trying to embrace for change, had been continually undermined by criticism. Her environment and her hopes were incompatible. One or the other eventually had to go.

That isn't quite the end of the story. About a year after her therapy was terminated, she scheduled an appointment to see me again. After a brief exchange of pleasantries, she burst our with: " ___ (ex-husband) and I are together again." My heart sank. She had come so far. She had made some enormous strides in her life. I was possessive of the progress she had made and didn't want to see her put that at risk. Of course, I didn't say all of that, but just listened to the story.

They were dating and trying to decide how, or if, they should pursue reconciling their marriage at this point. They wanted to know if I would see them together again and help with the process. I agreed to a meeting to help assess the situation and to see if I could help. It took me only about five minutes into the next meeting with both of them to want to throttle the guy.

He had in fact changed as he had represented to his former wife. He had become better at being subtle, indirect, and passive in his aggression toward her. The basic messages, however, were still the same: "You're kind of dumb," "You really haven't changed," "You still need me to keep you on track." I watched her listen to his "I've really changed" rhetoric and want to believe it, but then saw the wincing caution as she could hear the old themes emerge.

Eventually, she withdrew from the relationship. Not surprisingly, it was a difficult thing for her to do. The push to do so, however, came as she could feel the toxic nature of their interaction beginning to cloud the clearing view of her life that she had begun to discover. She understood the impossibility of living with the mutually exclusive dynamics of reaching for new perceptions, and living with a constant barrage of the old. She did make a difficult choice but has continued to enjoy the rewards of growth at a fair price.

Like many people, I have my accountant, my attorney, and a host of other professional resource people whose help I solicit from time to time. All of them have proven themselves well worth the time and money to consult on any number of issues and questions which come up occasionally. As important as their input may be, I have learned to qualify their advice. It became clear to me that of all of the major decisions I have made over the last several years, probably few would have been undertaken had I totally relied on any one of these important people. Why? Because their focus was exclusively on either risk or cost. They could not weigh the personal gain for me.

This raises an interesting point: Partial truth can undermine the most important undertakings and dreams in life. As I have mentioned, one of my most strongly felt passions is flying. There is absolutely no way that it makes any sense to own an airplane, if one asks the average non-pilot accountant. This has more to do with individual priorities than fiscal possibilities. It further makes little sense to have children; just think of the problems, not to mention the costs of medical care, wardrobe, college tuition, weddings, etc. Facts are facts. Thankfully they're not the only point of consideration. Don't judge others for their sense of values and priorities; don't let yourself be judged for yours. We cannot put our new life-enabling perceptions on the line to be assessed by those who have no experience with them nor value for them.

Faith does not disregard facts, nor does it give all of the decision-making power to them. Faith needs the consultative prudence of facts and information. It also needs the perspective that facts and information are based on what is known and experienced to date, and that those present benchmarks are only that — benchmarks of what has been demonstrated as possible up to this point, limited only by the vision, foresight, and faith of those dream undertakers. Remember, those benchmarks were once thought by those who now experience them as commonplace, to be entirely outside of the realm of possibility.

To exercise faith, to step outside of what is known for yourself or your world is to go through the inner and outer struggle of any pilgrim or adventurer. The great names in all civilizations were people of faith.

Whether we put that in religious terms or not is not particularly important. The unconventional have always tapped the inner spirit, created by the greater Spirit, to step into the unfamiliar land of something imagined. Realizing it or not, we all have our "God encounters" in inspiration, creative genius, great ideas, new visions, hope and peace. We often fail to recognize their source.

In the therapy business these are referred to as the "Ah hah!" experience. Some new awareness or insight barges into our perceptual world. I have sat and watched person after person touched in this way. It is like sitting on sacred ground, being privileged to watch the changing countenance reflective of a significant upheaval of perceptions. It is literally giving birth to not only new perceptions, but the inevitable end result of a different life direction. Of course, the choices made from that point on significantly affect the outcome, but the important thing is that the potential has been stimulated. The remaining task is to embrace the new perception of potential, at that time yet only faith, and tenaciously keep it as a point of focus.

Parents who loose sight of their goals in life sometimes hope to see them realized in their children. It is fine to want more for your kids, but the best way to facilitate that is to be one who models the process of faith born from healthy perceptions, being the vehicle to develop one's own life. Sometimes much of our struggle is due to the lack of good models. We can certainly be that for our children and those around us.

The price tag of faith is to be confronted by the reasons and fears about why it will not work. Faith has two sides. First is the commitment to a new perspective. Second is the tenacious embracing of that new perspective, and a refusal, in spite of current experiences, to let go, or glance away to the other seducing perspectives of fear, questions doubt — anything that suggests an outcome different than wanted. The point is, to act in faith is not to return to the original perspective or state. It allows the forward-moving energy to be modified as things and potentials become more clear; that does not imply rethinking, retracing, reconsidering. Faith says, "It will be different." It allows for adjustment, modification, refinement, but not return to the point of origin.

When we discuss the idea of faith being the "evidence of things not yet seen," it is helpful to capture a particular perception of the whole process. When I see someone take that first "step of faith" toward a goal or ambition, in my mind, from an outsider's perspective of the whole process, the matter is as good as done. To start, and to continue, is to finish. When we buy an airline ticket, we know where we're going to arrive; all we have to do is stay on board. When we sign up for an academic degree program, we know ahead of time what it will ultimately give us. The same is true of an act of faith toward any specific goal. To take that informed "leap" needs to be done with the awareness that the outcome is not in question, but is as real as that first step. There is only one criteria, tenacity. Stubborn even helps! The evidence of the outcome is in the beginning of the process; the outcome is not in question. That perspective on the operational side, the working out of one's faith, is essential to making the exercise of faith a foundation for realizing successful choices.

## *Summary*

Define for yourself the leap of faith you need to take toward a specific part of your life that you want to direct differently than it is now. Give yourself a specific time line as well, an hour, one day, something specific and *soon,* then do it.

## *Conclusion*

The mythology of our age is one that suggests the seductive idea of the absence of limitation to human potential. I was refreshed by a *Barbara Walters Special* some time ago, which included an interview with the actress Candice Bergen. Having enjoyed much success in her television role as Murphy Brown, and a focal point participant in national bantering over a "family values" commentary by our former Vice-President, she did have some surprising things to say. When asked about her view of the proclaimed "You-Can-Do-It-All Women," those able to manage career, marriage, children, and a personal life at the same time, she unflinchingly said, "I hate them!" Thankfully, she reflected an attitude of saneness about the ability of human beings to live for any length of time on the razor's edge of boundless excellence.

Of the many friends I have been blessed with over the years, an elderly gentleman fills my memory with warm thoughts while recalling some interesting conversations. In my earlier days of unbridled entrepreneurial spirit, enjoying the rush of exciting opportunities, he once said to me : "Ray, you can't marry all the girls." I agree that all of us use far less of our abilities and gifts than we possess. It is another matter however to suggest that doing it all is in our best interests. That attempt is, I believe, a gesture to bolster self esteem by performing to the standards of a neurotic system of values, ie, bigger is better, more is best, and he who dies with the most toys wins, etc.

The degree to which we are successfully managing those necessarily different parts of our lives is reflected in the degree of balance we are demonstrating. Balance implies that all components and factors are working in harmony, or at least not jeopardizing one another. That one value does not become so out of balance that it jeopardizes the function or existence of another. This is the demonstration of effective living.

If we are to have a significant degree of success in the management of our feelings, and the perceptions they give rise to, we are called to learn about the source of feelings, how they are fed, how they can be directed, and when they need to be discarded. Feelings are not good or bad; they are simply feelings. Feelings do not necessarily represent the truth; they often, in fact, distort truth to the degree of unrecognizability. Feelings can be a friend, to color, add breadth, and give rich dimension to our experience in life.

Choices are the vehicle of privilege. Regardless of the appearances, or realities, of anyone's situation, there are choices to be made. They may have limits, there may be realistic constraints, *but there are choices available!* Those choices include what actions are available, what time allows, what experience provides, and *at least,* how we will choose to look at the events or opportunities presenting themselves to us.

Perceptions are chosen ways to view anything from how we feel to what we define as the meaning of an experience. That becomes a position which profoundly affects how we approach, respond, and ultimately interplay with our experiences in day-to-day living, to accomplishing something of importance.

There is always more to say than what we have been able to address in this book. There is the hope that what has been said is sufficient to communicate what has demonstrated itself to be of importance about this inner world of perceptions. The awareness of the different choices and views we have available to us in any situation is, I believe, a great tool. Making those choices consistently will, with sometimes great effort, create anything from some small measurable change, to something profoundly different in the way we live. Life and change don't have to be as difficult as we sometimes make them.

The fact that you have purchased and read this book indicates that you are a person who needs no invitation to personal growth. I hope that this book provides for you a stimuli for an additional set of tools to make everyday life easier to manage, and the dreams you have, easier to realize.

To contact **Dr. Ray Watson** for speaking or training programs he may be reached at the address or phone number below.

To order additional copies of
## Putting Power In Your Perceptions

Please send ____ copies at $14.95 for each book, plus $3.50 shipping and handling for the first book, $2 for each additional book.

Enclosed is my check or money order of $_____
or [ ] Visa   [ ] MasterCard
#_____ Exp. Date _____/_____
Signature _____
Phone _____

Name _____
Street Address _____
City _____
State _____ Zip _____

(Advise if recipient and mailing address are different from above.)

### For credit card orders call:
### 1-800-RJW-0552
### 1-800-759-0552

or

Return this order form to:

### RJW Publications
P.O. Box 40190
Bellevue, Washington 98015-4190